To Jennie
With Love,
Vanessa

Forever Home Within

VANESSA BUNTING

BALBOA.
PRESS

A DIVISION OF HAY HOUSE

Balboa Press books may be ordered through booksellers or by contacting:

Balboa Press
A Division of Hay House
1663 Liberty Drive
Bloomington, IN 47403
www.balboapress.com
1 (877) 407-4847

Because of the dynamic nature of the Internet, any web addresses or
links contained in this book may have changed since publication and
may no longer be valid. The views expressed in this work are solely those
of the author and do not necessarily reflect the views of the publisher,
and the publisher hereby disclaims any responsibility for them.

The author of this book does not dispense medical advice or prescribe
the use of any technique as a form of treatment for physical, emotional,
or medical problems without the advice of a physician, either directly
or indirectly. The intent of the author is only to offer information
of a general nature to help you in your quest for emotional and
spiritual well-being. In the event you use any of the information in
this book for yourself, which is your constitutional right, the author
and the publisher assume no responsibility for your actions.

Any people depicted in stock imagery provided by Thinkstock are
models, and such images are being used for illustrative purposes only.
Certain stock imagery © Thinkstock.

Printed in the United States of America.

ISBN: 978-1-4525-8597-0 (sc)
ISBN: 978-1-4525-8598-7 (e)

Balboa Press rev. date: 2/11/2014

For anyone who needs a hug right now.

Acknowledgements

To my husband, Tony, for allowing me the time and freedom I needed to write this book.

Also to my wonderful sisters: Ann, Trish, and Liz, and to their families, who have listened with interest to my ramblings about this book, as have my friends Jackie, Abi, Pam, Doris and David.

Special thanks to Gill, who held my hand and reassured me during my darkest days – without you, my dear friend, I might never have left the house.

The many managers over the years who gave me opportunities and skills: Alan, Graham, John, Neal, Linda, and Philip.

For Annie & Barrie who stayed at our house and looked after our pets so well over many years which enabled us to take holidays.

Emma, your interest and encouragement in this book helped me complete it.

And to my mum and all the people and animals who have passed on before but still stay firmly in my heart and mind.

I thank you all.

Preface

Forever Home Within is a simple but insightful read about the trials I found whilst living alone. Initially my home was the most important thing in my life, along with various cats, dogs, and romances over the years. But eventually, after almost 20 years, I finally realized that a move to a truly beautiful cottage just wasn't my dream anymore. This book hasn't been about logging life's events so much as describing the life of someone who has thoughts and feelings some people may relate to and take comfort from. There is no need for anyone to feel alone these days, and a few simple anecdotes from someone who understands might make all the difference. To put things into context, I found new beginnings by making changes in my life, basing decisions upon instincts and honesty, to help fulfil that innermost place – that *Forever Home Within*.

Contents

Chapters:

Illustrations:

Front Cover: Rosie
Rear Cover: Romie

1

Birth to Sixteen

I was born in December 1960. Mum had been in hospital all over Christmas waiting for me to arrive, and I made my appearance two weeks late. Then I promptly contracted whooping cough, so I had a further stay in hospital until I was well enough to leave. It might not have been the best start in life, but as a baby, I obviously wasn't aware of much, unlike Mum. She was less than pleased at having another girl (the fourth after her son); she had handed me to my dad, saying, "You name her." And so he did.

Although I was the youngest child, I was never a favourite. I don't think Mum and Dad had favourites – in fact, they saw to it that we were never spoilt in any way. We did have fun times, though. Mum used to play a game with me when I was a little tot: I would sit on her lap with my legs astride, facing her, and she'd bounce me up and down, holding my hands and singing a little song while whistling a bit. I just had to listen out for the word *bagpipes*, because then her legs would open, and I'd fall through the gap! I thought this was hilarious and always wanted more, until Mum would finally say, "No, that's enough now."

Her word was final; it always was where we were concerned – but less so where Dad featured. During my preschool years, I'd wait at the front gate for Dad to come home from work. He would scoop me up and put me on the saddle of his huge push-bike, and I would hold his arm as he pushed me up the path, around the side of the house, and through another gate. It felt as if I were sitting on a mountain, it was so high up, but then I was probably only a couple of feet tall at the time.

It was generally understood in our three-bedroomed semi-detached council house that parents knew best by virtue of the fact that they were much older and more worldly-wise, so their instructions or decisions were never questioned by their five children. It wasn't a carrot-and-stick approach, either, as there were no carrots – just the serious threat of a stick, although I cannot remember any one of us being smacked.

I started at the nearby infant school when I was either 5 or 6 years old. I could already write a small amount of words but quickly decided I didn't want to learn any more amidst a classroom full of strangers. So come lunchtime, I left a note on the teacher's desk which said I had gone home – or words to that effect. The next thing I knew, the teacher had come to my house and taken me back to school. There I was to wait until my Mum picked me up, and when she did, she was furious. She almost dragged me home. She actually came out with the classic cliché "Wait till your father gets home!" She sent me straight to bed without tea, and I cried until I heard Dad come in and Mum's voice droning on as she told him all about it.

After a while, Dad came up the stairs, opened the door, and quietly asked, "Why did you leave school today?"

I can't remember my answer, which was probably something like "I didn't like it." He just said, "Don't do it again." He closed the door as he left. I didn't do it again.

Strangely enough, there didn't appear to be any real interest from our parents regarding our schooling. School reports were duly read by both, but that's as far as it went – there was no attendance for parents' evenings or sports days. This was largely due to them both working and not having the time, or rather not *making* the time.

Once, in the cookery class, the teacher asked who wanted to make a plain Christmas cake and who wanted to make a fancy one. I opted for the plain and, after getting into the respective groups, we got on with the cake over the following weeks. As we neared the icing stage, I knew I wouldn't be getting any sparkly ribbons or frosted trees from home, so I thought carefully about how I would decorate it. I made little icing holly leaves and berries, which I arranged in the centre of the square cake, and then I piped lines of lattice across each corner before piping waves of icing around the top edge and bottom onto the silver cake board. I then very carefully piped hanging loops around the whole cake, which slightly overlapped, giving a further loop and detail.

As I finished, I realized the whole class and teacher were watching me. The teacher then said, "Vanessa, why did you say you were making a plain cake, when you should have been in the fancy group?" I wanted to cry and quietly said that I had intended it to be plain. The teacher was not annoyed with me at all; on the contrary, she praised my efforts. She had the whole class over to see my cake. I think I was as surprised as they were, and more so when she wanted it displayed in the school's main entrance hall with a few other cakes. There it stayed for a few weeks, with my name card in front of it.

The strangest thing is, any pride that I had was wiped out by the feeling of complete embarrassment. I cringed every time I saw it with my name with it. I wanted to be invisible, an unknown. Here my name and efforts were on show for all to see. When I took the cake home, the emphasis shifted immediately to what it would taste like rather than look like, and thankfully, it didn't disappoint. There was no place for vanity or ego in our house.

The school used to host the cycling proficiency training and testing, and somehow I found myself cycling around the playground with a load of strangers as part of this instruction. There were several children from other schools, and one such boy, David, took a shine to me, for some reason, and would try to talk to me. I was very shy and didn't want to be "chatted up" or particularly to get to know him, but this was one young lad who didn't have a faint heart and wasn't going to give up easily!

He followed me home on his bike. I pedalled home as fast as I could and felt almost panic-stricken by the time I'd got indoors. He just sat outside on his bike. The family thought it was hilarious and taunted me, saying, "Ness, your boyfriend's waiting outside for you. Go and talk to him." I sat at the top of the stairs and had no intention of going anywhere. This happened a few times – by today's standards he might have been called a stalker. Luckily, the cycling proficiency test came and went, and I think poor David took the hint that he was indeed going to have to *get on his bike* where I was concerned.

As children, we used to joke among ourselves that we were latchkey kids, because our parents were usually still out at work when we came home from school. On one particular occasion, I was the first home. We always used the back door, which was at the side of the house. The front door was for visitors, tradesmen, and letting the dog out – yes, he used to roam free sometimes and come and scratch at the front door to be let in. How irresponsible was that?

Anyway, I had come home and got on with lighting the Rayburn range in the lounge. After laying the paper and kindling, I realized there were no matches, so I went back up the lounge, through the hall and into the kitchen, and took a light from the gas cooker with a rolled-up piece of paper. By the time I'd got to the hall, I knew the paper was too short to reach the lounge, so I doubled back and put it in the sink. This time I rolled up a really long piece of newspaper so it would last the journey to the fire, but by the time I'd got to the hall again, I had a huge inferno at the end of my hand, so naturally I dropped it. I had the presence of mind to smother the flames with a garment I'd snatched from the ironing basket which lived behind the kitchen door. I jumped up to stamp the fire out; I was shaking like a leaf. Then I noticed that the garment I had used was Dad's blue cotton shirt, which now had a hole in the back and was burnt around the edge!

Amazingly, no one else had yet come home. Equally amazingly, the hall mat wasn't showing signs of damage, probably because it was in various shades of brown. I couldn't risk going to the dustbin to dump the shirt, in case I bumped into someone on their way in, so I scrunched up the shirt and put it at the bottom of the ironing pile, until it was safe to put it in the bin. In the interests of self-preservation, ruining Dad's shirt while almost burning the house down was definitely going to be my secret!

I was aware that my home life was different from many. There was nothing unusual about Dad liking country and western music (although some may beg to differ) or frequenting his local pub, the Crooked Billet, for a social pint or five. Yes, it has to be said that Dad liked a drink – mostly beer, but he would sometimes have spirit chasers. He didn't like having alcohol in the house, but said that the village pub and socializing were both essential, and he simply couldn't resist a visit. He used this excuse on holiday when we went to various static caravan sites in Kent. He would always check out the nearest pub while Mum would wait with the rest of us on a pebbly beach (sometimes a tarry pebbly beach, if there had been an oil spill) until he returned with a fish-and-chip lunch. Sometimes Mum would get in a mood over this (quite understandably), but then Dad would shout her down, and we kids would be annoyed with Mum for setting Dad off. Happy holidays!

Ironically, at Christmas alcohol was drunk in the home (as well as the pub) and we always had the flap down on the stereogram to act as a shelf. The whole lot was covered in a Christmas-paper tablecloth, and there'd be beer and spirits aplenty, punctuated by bowls of Satsuma oranges and mixed nuts (nuts you cracked yourself with nutcrackers that looked like pliers). As a special treat, once a year, we were allowed a sherry glass of Stone's Ginger Wine – and how we savoured that special privilege as well as the warming sweet fluid.

When he wasn't working his various shifts on the railway, Dad spent much time digging around his allotment near our home – in fact, it was near the pub, too. There were times when I'd watch him from the window as he sped towards home. He reminded me of John Wayne in looks and size, and had he been riding a horse instead of a bike, he'd have been a dead ringer.

I learned that it was possible to tell from the colour of his face whether he'd been to the allotment or the pub after work. Basically, the redder the face the more likely it was that he'd been to the pub, and this could be good or bad. We might get a good-humoured Dad, home with a pocketful of chocolate bars and nut rings, with the shake of his hand on our heads as he dished them out (it was his way of saying that he loved us, and we knew this without the kissing or the word *love* ever being mentioned in our house. Mind you, I did kiss our black Labrador dog, Jock, and told him I loved him – and meant it!) On the other hand, we might get a bad-tempered man who would find something to shout about as soon as he got through the back door. He would bellow, "Who's left those bikes out the front?" (or boots, or toys, etc.) or "Why haven't those rabbits been fed?" (or the dog walked – even if they had.) If we weren't all there to answer to the misdemeanour, we'd have to explain where the missing one was, knowing they'd get the same earful when they got in. We just accepted that our place, as children, was at the bottom of the pecking order, and we were normally responsible for getting on adults' nerves.

Mum was far from exempt; in fact, she was more likely to be in the line of fire. Where she was concerned, Dad's rage could turn to violence. This was very distressing to us all, but our cries did nothing to deter him. How Mum kept her sanity, let alone her patience with him, I'll never know. She already had her hands full with one son, four daughters, a part-time job in a dairy – which she didn't particularly like – and our pet dog, which she liked even less. It was the way she kept her cool and emotions in check that made me realize I would never in all my life be remotely like her in accepting this treatment from anyone.

Even the death of their eldest child, my brother Stephen, had not united them. Stephen suddenly died at the age of just 20. I was nine at the time and was told the news by my eldest sister. Because we were children, we were not allowed to attend Stephen's funeral, and we didn't discuss his death in our family; we just somehow got through it with the occasional discreet weeping, prompting a hug from a sister. It may seem strange, but I didn't know Stephen that well. I do know he was quiet and gentle, artistic and kind; he went to work, went to church, and played cricket. I couldn't understand why he had his own bedroom while we four girls were crammed into one room together.

I used to hear Stephen praying in his room sometimes, and when I didn't hear him praying, I used to knock on his door and ask if he had any odd coppers. He'd disappear for a few seconds and then hand over a handful of coppers, which I'd go and put straight in my piggy bank. (Well, it wasn't a piggy bank, as such, but a sitting dog with a slit in his head – nice!) So it was no surprise that I missed my very special brother, and my tears would flow uncontrollably.

I never once saw my parents cry, even through this. Mum was probably consumed with constant worry to the point of numbness, and she seemed to use her cool detachment to cope with her son's death in very much the same way.

A while after Stephen died, I boldly approached Mum and Dad in the kitchen one Sunday morning and asked if I could have Stephen's bedroom. To my surprise, they agreed straight away, and before I knew it, they had the bed made and my clothes in the drawers, and I had the start of a new independence. My sisters didn't seem to mind; they were probably glad of the extra space in their room.

It was about this time that Mum took three of us on the train to Faversham in Kent to stay with my Aunt Mary and Uncle Lionel (my Mum's brother). We had two cousins too, Catherine and James, who were a little older than me, and they made us very welcome. They lived in a modest-sized Victorian detached cottage with whitewashed walls and a tall chimney stack at one gable end. The front door was just short of the pathway on the main road and was seldom used. A tall hedge ran along the boundary of the property, and the main access was via a country lane off the main road, and through a large white gate to a shingled car-park area. From there, a single brick pathway led through the lawned garden right to the back door. The garden actually wrapped right around the house. Although narrow at the front, it housed a wooden barn/stable block to one side, with chickens and a paddock, and to the other side of the garden lay a well-tended vegetable garden and flower beds.

This place was beautiful, and the biggest plus point for me was the three horses they owned. This meant that I could go riding for free, groom the horses, saddle the horses, talk about the horses again and again – yes,

I was in horsey heaven! Admittedly, my sisters weren't quite as enthusiastic about the horses, but Liz and Trish were able to indulge in their passion for cooking and cake making with Aunt Mary, so they enjoyed their "holiday" too. We probably stayed only for a week at a time, but it always seemed longer to me, and it was a real holiday. Apart from the fantastic experience of those breaks away, I think the cottage itself and the gentle and peaceful family life there played a large part in influencing our outlook and aspirations, even if only subconsciously at that time.

One by one, through the 1970s my teenage sisters found love in their lives. They all married young and left home to start families of their own. There were early indications that I wasn't going to do the same, as my love was placed firmly with Jock, our dog (I don't know why we named him that). He was Border collie crossed with a black Labrador owned by our next-door neighbour and given to us as a puppy. He was mostly black but had a white bib and white paws. On the end of his tail he had a single white hair. With Jock I'd walk for miles, taking hours, through the beautiful and contrasting countryside surrounding our home. This ranged from the driest and brightest expanse of cornfields to damp and dense woodlands filled with ancient trees swathed in moss and tangled brambles. It was the real sense of inner peace and comfort I found in this outside world that was the most rewarding for me. I felt completely fearless, as children often are, and thankfully no harm ever came to me.

My love of animals and nature was encouraged by Dad, who would sometimes come and watch me riding at a local riding school. This was where I'd spend my savings and pocket money earned from jobs like going to the shops or sweeping up hedge trimmings in the front garden. Dad would also make wooden animal toys, with excellent precision and detail. He made my wooden hobby horse, which I absolutely loved. I don't know what happened to it; I wish I'd kept it, but I did keep a large wooden stable and tack room he made for my Sindy horse and Thunderbolt, which I still have today.

Dad was also a keen gardener, and he used his allotment to grow a whole host of vegetables for family and friends. Also, a neighbour had given us three chickens, white leghorns, which we named Henny, Clara, and Gerty. Dad sectioned off a third of the garden with a chicken coop and run, which he put together in no time. Apart from the corn we threw down for them, the chickens seemed to survive on scratching around for food all day, and they got really big, as did their eggs, which were often double yoked. I remember taking some eggs for the cookery teacher at school, and she thought I was winding her up by bringing her duck eggs!

It was always exciting to see that the chickens had laid eggs in their straw-laden box, and of course they were completely organic and free range. I loved the chickens. They slept on their low perch in the coop, and whoever was in the middle (normally Clara) would put her wings out slightly over the other two so it looked as if they were cuddling up together for the night.

Dad did care about animals, and if it hadn't been for his drinking, he could have been a brilliant man, as he had so many good qualities and skills. Unfortunately, through his drinking, his unpredictable Jekyll-and-Hyde character made it difficult to completely trust or respect him.

Years later, when I was the only child at home, I'd taken a few exams and was due to leave school. Dad sat me down and told me firmly that if I didn't get a job I'd have to leave, as I wasn't going to be sponging off them. He told me that he'd never claimed a penny off the state in his life and he didn't expect me to, either. I didn't know if he was serious about throwing me out, but I figured that either way I needed money, so within two weeks of leaving school I'd secured a job in a marine insurance underwriting room in the City of London. It didn't pay much, and I was mostly making drinks and photocopying, but I did enjoy the atmosphere and took an interest in all the various shipping disasters at sea. I used to write about them sometimes and attach the newspaper clippings – the massive oil spill from the Amoco Cadiz springs to mind as being one. I compiled a little folder for myself, which I still have today, as Mum kept it for years.

Like the ships I had been dealing with, I was heading towards stormy seas, because my parents now started divorce proceedings after thirty years of marriage. I'm surprised their marriage lasted so long.

I suppose it was not the "done" thing to get divorced in those days, and where children were involved there was always the misconception that a family needed to include both parents. With my sisters gone, this was no longer the case.

As individuals, Mum and Dad were like chalk and cheese. They had different values, expectations, and political and religious beliefs, and they came from different backgrounds. I remember Dad belonging to the Communist Party, and he'd have his mates come to the house – they looked to me like gangsters. They used to call him Comrade, and I used to think, "That's not his name." Now I would be moving out with mum. I'd hoped it wouldn't have an effect on my work, but I had to go to court to testify to Dad's unreasonable behaviour. This I found very difficult, as he was still my father, but it was a legal requirement. I was also assured by the court that my employers would receive a letter to explain my absence in this respect. I got back to work one day to be told that, while it wasn't my fault that I had to keep appearing in court, it wasn't theirs, either, and they promptly sacked me. I was really upset and sat at my desk crying.

I knew then that this seemed like unfair dismissal and I could fight my employer's decision, but I'd seen enough of courtrooms already, so I set about finding another job instead. Obviously Mum and Dad were too busy sorting out splitting up and accommodation issues to sympathise with me. I just went about my business with a certain amount of urgency. My main concern was how I was to explain to a potential employer at the interview that I'd been sacked from my previous job.

I needn't have worried. An agency had sent me to an interview at another insurance company in the same street in London, where I was honest and open about the situation. I explained that domestic problems had gotten in the way of my attendance, but that all the issues were resolved now. Apparently it was my honesty and the twelve months' experience in an underwriting room which got me the job as an office assistant. The academic requirement was A-level standard (not mine), but I soon learned the ropes, and my salary was almost doubled from the start.

The only pet we had left at home was the dog, and saying goodbye to Jock was, for me, the most upsetting aspect of leaving. My much-loved pet was now 16 and on his last legs, literally. Dad had gone to work the morning we left, and as Mum and I left the house, Jock was barking at the window constantly, as if he knew we wouldn't be back and I'd never see him again. I never did. He died from a heart attack a few months later.

2

Seventeen to Nineteen

Everyone tends to have an especially significant year in his or her life, and for me it was the summer of 1978. This was the year when I started looking forward to the future with optimism and high hopes. It was the first time in my seventeen years that I could honestly describe my home life as stable, job prospects as feasible, good friends plenty, and anything else as just brilliant!

Now Mum and I were as free as birds, and we moved into a newly built, stylish two-bedroomed flat at Crystal Palace, South London. Mum had acquired the flat through a housing association. Now we had the opportunity to really get to know each other and start a new life. We soon turned the flat into a lovely, comfortable home, which was airy yet cosy, with the bare essentials we managed to salvage from the house in Kent. (Dad had locked many of their shared possessions in the shed before going to work on the day we left.)

The two blocks of flats were only two storeys high. They overlooked a terrace of beautifully kept Victorian houses. Despite being in London, there was a real sense of community here, and it was not unusual to see the same friendly faces to say hello to in the local shops. To the rear of the flats was a pretty landscaped communal garden, retained by a low wall which kept it separate from the small car park and washing-line area for the residents.

We moved in during a warm summer, and after a couple of weeks to get settled (I know it was a hundred times harder for Mum to adapt to the single life), we went about starting our new respective jobs. Mum went by bus to the Post Office 10 miles away and I made a twenty-minute train ride to an insurance company in the city. The term *duck to water* would be an understatement, as I just loved the buzz of this new life. In no time I had made many new friends at work. It was a very "young" office with a very understanding and noise-tolerant boss.

I didn't really know the meaning of hard work in those days, so I would spend my boundless energy dancing away the night at various clubs. The only thing holding me back was the lack of cash, because housekeeping money to Mum was really important now, as there were just the two of us. This wasn't a problem though, and I couldn't complain, as Mum always cooked me lovely meals and paid all the bills. It was obvious that Mum was happy now too, because all the subordination and fear in her life had been replaced by the enjoyment of the simplest things, like being able to say, "What do you fancy for dinner this weekend?" or "Darling, I've brought some tomato plants to grow on the balcony." On this occasion we both laughed when I sarcastically pointed out that the balcony was *never* in sunlight and it would be impossible to grow anything out there – I'd have been out there sunbathing if there was any chance of getting a tan! So there was no way tomatoes would be growing there.

"Oh well," said Mum with a smile, "the foliage is very pretty and will brighten the balcony anyway. I can buy tomatoes from the shops!"

Dear, sweet Mum, with her short, wavy auburn hair and small build, was always there making the best of every situation. She didn't mind when I stayed out late enjoying myself and lapping up all the male attention, because she knew this was sheer freedom to me. At 19 years of age, I didn't have a care in the world.

Apart from the usual shopping and scouting around local markets during weekends, Mum and I would go into the garden, where we'd meet up with some of our very friendly and interesting neighbours. The most significant were Vicki and Cyril, a middle-aged couple full of fun who, surprisingly, had no children yet adored their two cats, Kiki and Sheba. Vicki reminded me in looks of the actress Pat Coombs, and Cyril, with his white hair, curly moustache, and colourful cravats, was often likened by people to the actor Howard Keel. But these two were indeed stars in their own right, with big personalities, kind hearts, and ready humour. Then there were Abigail and David, a trendy pair a few years older than myself, who lived together next door with their black cat, Felix.

We became a regular group of folk in the garden, whether it was a summer evening during the working week or a Sunday afternoon. We took turns to make cups of tea and provide delicious cakes, such as my favourites, chocolate fudge and Victoria sponge, which were mostly home-made. Mum made excellent cakes, but I spared everyone my efforts and went for shop-bought every time. This became a very enjoyable ritual for us all, rather than a boring routine. Our conversations were always so light-hearted and easy – seldom negative but sometimes bitchy, if the story required. It's fair to say that our time spent in that little patch of paradise gave us all true relaxation, irrespective of age or background, wants or needs.

Within these few years at work, I learned that there was to be a large profit-share pay-out to staff, so Mum and I decided to take ourselves off on holiday somewhere hot. It was very fortunate that Mum had a sister who lived in the Caribbean, in Barbados. What's more, the sisters hadn't seen each other in ages. What an opportunity this was, because not only had I never met my Aunt Kath and Uncle Stuart, but this was to be the first time either of us had been on an aeroplane.

It was 1980, and we got a brilliant deal from the renowned Laker Airlines (although in retrospect the prices today are probably lower). I had been packing since the moment I knew we were going away, and when I wasn't packing, I was busy writing lists of all the things I was *going* to pack. The excitement was almost too much to bear. Finally, after what seemed like endless waiting, we set off for our holiday of a lifetime – three weeks in glorious sunshine.

Being on a jumbo jet felt great, and listening to disco music on the headset made me want to bop about in my seat and start to party already! Mum took it all in her stride, although I knew she was apprehensive about the whole thing. She was now the responsible adult in the relationship, without the security of a husband to lean on if anything went wrong.

We arrived over Barbados at night, and after a ten-hour flight, we had to circle while the crew waited for permission to land. I was thinking what an excellent sensation it was to be banked over, circling the island and seeing tiny lights everywhere, some scattered, some clustered, but all magical and signifying that our dream holiday island was just below. Mum's attitude wasn't quite the same, and I could see she would have been happier on a white-knuckle ride at a fairground than this!

After landing, we left the plane and made our way into the steamy, humid chaos inside the tiny airport. Despite the darkness of night, the airport temperature was very hot and not at all conducive to queuing with hundreds of other passengers in order to get through customs. We had already waited ages for our luggage to appear on the equally slow carousel. Little did I know that this experience was to mark the norm for many future foreign trips, regardless of location or time of day – I was up for anything!

Eventually we emerged, none the worse, to warm smiles and lengthy embraces from Aunt Kath and Uncle Stuart. This journey, in all senses of the word, was a very important turning point for Mum. Not only did it represent her new independence, but for the first time she could finally take consolation with the sister who, coincidentally, had also tragically lost her son, Michael, in his youth, around the same time as Stephen's passing. Now at last came a sharing of hearts and minds, a giving of love and support which had been so long overdue.

For me *holiday mode* was the only approach I had, which meant heading for that soft, white sandy beach every day in order to get a *serious* tan. Unfortunately, there was no escaping the hard sell of the locals, with their briefcases stuffed with coral jewellery and gifts – even if you *were* lying down with your face covered by a sun hat and ears by headsets! "A beautiful coral necklace for a beautiful lady?" was a sound that was all too familiar. I'd sometimes want to say what was really on my mind, but I always chose a curt "no thanks" instead.

Mum chilled very well. One day she surprised me by saying, "Well, I wouldn't mind having my photograph taken with *him*." I looked around and saw a small, lean Bajan man, who I didn't really think was Mum's type. However, there's no accounting for taste, so I went up and politely asked the man if he'd mind posing with Mum for a photo. He was very obliging and stood bolt upright, with a beaming, if awkward, smile as he placed his arm around Mum's shoulder. Mum, on the other hand, stood rigid, with a look of total embarrassment and worry on her face. I took the photo, and we both thanked the man, who went off quite happy that he'd made someone's day. Then Mum turned to me and said through her gritted teeth, "I didn't mean *him* – I meant *him*!" and nodded her head towards a tall Scandinavian-looking hunk! We both laughed – loudly and for a very long time.

After two weeks – thanks to our brilliant hosts, who had arranged, advised, driven, and collected us everywhere – we had "done" the beaches, shops, bars, restaurants, and Jolly Roger boat trip (from which we both returned worse for wear due to the free-flowing rum punch on board). We had had the *yin* of our holiday, but now it looked as though the final week was going to be the *yang*, as a radio broadcaster casually announced that Hurricane Allen was on its way to the Caribbean at a speed of 150 mph. Of course, Kath and Stuart were used to these situations, so we had planned nothing more than a night in with a few board games on the evening of the anticipated strike.

Mum and I opted for the basement "sewing room" for an early night of serious praying (I became suddenly religious) and sharing a half bottle of Scotch. Fortunately sleep, or sheer unconsciousness, took over during the hurricane bombardment, which we learned in the morning had veered north at the last minute. Even so, the devastation was obvious – there were masses of small wooden boats washed up and damaged on the coastal roads and millions of palm leaves appeared to be stuck on just about everything we saw. The prospect of going home wasn't so bad after all. We were both looking forward to seeing friends again, and indeed family, as my sisters didn't live far away from us and we regularly kept in touch.

It was good to be back. At work the boss gave me the whole day to talk about my holiday. He had obviously hoped that this would get it all out of my system so I wouldn't be distracting other staff for the rest of the week.

It was also great to see Vicki, Cyril, and Abigail (David had moved out). I spent more and more time with Vicki and Cyril, who treated me like their own daughter, and I treated them like parents. In turn, Abigail spent time with my mum, who treated her like a daughter, which I really didn't mind. However, without realizing it, Mum and I had started to grow apart. This, strangely, turned out to be a blessing in disguise. There's no point going into all the various scenarios that ensued, as they would provide neither clarity nor interest, I'm sure. Suffice it to say that I began to resent Mum's attitude towards my spending time with Vicki and Cyril, although I know that I should have been more understanding and less selfish. The blessing in disguise came as an announcement at work that our department was to move to Essex, and the request came for as many staff as possible to move too. Had I not had this blip with Mum, I would have considered the office move long and hard and might have opted against it. But as it stood, it looked like a fantastic opportunity, one to be seized with both hands.

There were very attractive financial benefits and costs paid, which would give me a real chance to spread my wings once more and make a new life in another place. The big, wide world out there had not let me down so far, so this was surely the right move for me.

Mum was naturally upset by this news, but a very quick six weeks later we parted on good terms. We had spent a few eventful and truly enjoyable years together – not long enough to get to really know each other, but long enough, it seemed. Of course we would keep in touch, as I would also with Vicki, Cyril, and Abigail, who had left shortly after I did to become an air stewardess in the Middle East.

Mum and I in Barbados

3

Twenty to Twenty-Six

As it turned out, there were only a handful of us who moved to Essex, but I was lucky to find, fifteen miles from where I'd be working, a very pleasant two-bedroomed flat in a small block overlooking fields. To me this meant countryside, and it was really good to see again, as it reminded me of my childhood in Kent. I moved in with my large tabby cat, Winston.

The new office was very easy to settle into, particularly as my job was the same as before, and there were a few familiar faces. The unfamiliar faces were friendly anyway, which meant even more potential friends.

Life's simple pleasures came to the fore once more, with me pottering around the flat and home-making, one of my favourite things. This was largely due to very limited funds. I planned my shopping list very carefully or, as Mum would say, "cut my coat to fit the cloth". I did enjoy the weekly mooch around the market to buy cheap, but fresh, fruit and vegetables, and then I would go to the butcher's for meat for the stews, curries, and casseroles which would keep me happy and healthy for another week or two. After payday I would extend the shopping to buy something new for the flat, be it potpourri, rose oil, plants, pots, or pictures. I seldom brought records now or new clothes, and as for the disco nights, well, they were currently "suspended until further notice", and I accepted this as part of the deal.

Mum came to visit occasionally, as did Vicki, Cyril, and Abigail, but unfortunately, they never came over together, even though I had enough room and suggested it. It was great when we did meet up; I always arranged a day trip to one of the many little villages in the county, where we'd stop for a drink and a bite to eat at a pub or tea shop. In an effort to relive days gone by, we'd shop in the local town and then go and sit in the flat's communal garden for our afternoon tea (although this one was less communal garden and more square piece of grassland flanked on two sides by flats). Sometimes the other neighbours would come out and join us or simply say hi while passing by. Whenever possible I went back to London to see everyone, including my sisters and nephews and nieces, who were ever increasing in numbers and height.

I regularly sat outside in the communal garden, and sure enough, I found new friends who, like me, were also young and rather noisy. Once, having got permission from the management company, I arranged a summer barbecue and charged a meagre £2 per ticket, saying, "All welcome, and bring your own drinks". This decision had stemmed from disco-withdrawal syndrome. I stuck some posters in each block of flats to advertise the event, borrowed tables and chairs from a local school, and then sorted out a barbecue and cooking duties with friends.

It was lovely to see more than thirty people turn up, with plenty of alcohol. The evening itself was warm following a hot, sunny day; there was plenty of food, which was going down well, and with the music coming from the stereo strategically placed at my lounge window, a good time was inevitable. Many new friendships were formed that night.

Many of us said we'd love to do it again, but predictably it just didn't come about. Despite my new-found sense of community, I still experienced a few niggles. There were inconveniences which I hadn't experienced while living in London. There was the more-than-occasional petty theft of washing from the communal line; the gas cylinder for my heater was stolen from right outside the front door; I was robbed of my motorcycle (I had purchased it as a cheap travel option); then, having borrowed a friend's motorcycle, I had parts of that stolen, too!

The motorbike situation came about quite strangely, considering my conversation with a school friend, Jo, when I'd first moved into the flat. Jo used to come over and stay sometimes, and we'd always incorporate going to a nightclub on the Saturday night, to "boogie on down", as we used to say. I had loads of 12-inch disco records, which we'd play while getting ready. In fact, Jo met her future husband at one of the clubs; they went on to marry, have children, and live happily ever after. Anyway, when Jo had phoned in those early days, she had asked if there was any "talent" in the area, to which I'd laughed and said something to the effect that they were all heavy-metal merchants with motorbikes. Little did I know that a few years down the line *I'd* become one of them!

In fact, my music tastes changed too, and I was well into rock, all of a sudden, as well as beer drinking. Needless to say, I didn't see Jo much after my metamorphosis. I did learn to ride, through a local school, and I passed my test so I could ride my blue Kawasaki 250 cc Scorpion, which was great!

Fortunately, just before the second theft, I had whizzed down to London to see Mum, having been prompted by a telephone conversation with her. She seemed unusually down in the dumps and mentioned how dowdy her kitchen was looking. This wasn't like Mum at all, as she was usually so happy-go-lucky. Probably the kitchen was okay, but it was an excuse for her to mope. In any event, I stopped off en route and brought some cheap, but nice-looking, kitchen wallpaper I thought she'd like. The paper was a blue-and-white pattern, really lovely and fresh looking. Mum's units were white, so they'd match perfectly well. I just about fitted everything into my already-full rucksack, including the paste (I trusted Mum had the brushes and bucket, and I knew I could use the dining room table to paste on). Such was the weight on the back that I'm sure if it hadn't been for the handlebars to hold onto, I'd have toppled over backwards! It must have been a funny sight.

It was lovely to see Mum again, and I really enjoyed decorating her kitchen, which was not only a massive improvement but, more importantly, cheered Mum enormously. We both knew I was there because I loved her and didn't want her to feel alone and down (which could have also been attributed to Vicki and Cyril's move to Sussex). Nevertheless, we spent a real mother-and-daughter time together, and by the time I left the next day, we both felt at ease with the world again.

Shortly after my visit, Mum met a good man, Ken, at the local tea dance where she helped out. Ken had popped in to see a friend while he was in the area from Hampshire, and – bingo – they spotted each other. Ken was to be her second husband. My sisters were as thrilled as I was that Mum's life had taken this wonderful turn. In no time, she and Ken had moved to Norfolk to enjoy their life together.

Things were looking up for us all, as I had met a very special man too. Mark was a friend of a neighbour. He was tall, fair, very handsome, and good company. We'd go to places on his motorbike, laugh, talk, and drink whatever took our fancy. However, after four months together, I noticed that while Mark did not drink excessively, his character did change – something with which I was all too familiar and, indeed, felt very insecure about. I ended things, rather reluctantly, but

I knew there were deep unresolved issues with Mark that were too heavy for me to understand at that time.

The following winter was freezing in that little flat. There was a single heater, which just about kept the damp at bay. The large, panoramic, single-glazed windows were wonderful for the light and views, but they did absolutely nothing for insulation. Money was still very tight, so I worked some evenings after work as a door-to-door canvasser selling (ironically) cavity wall insulation. With a few other equally desperate individuals, I walked for miles each evening in those three-hour stints. The money was negligible but for each lead we obtained came a few extra pounds.

Invariably the knocking on doors took us to all sorts of properties, with the obvious criterion that they all had cavity walls (shown by the bricks lying lengthways rather than long, short, long, short, etc.), a pretty easy aspect of the job to grasp, although this was altogether socially insightful. For a start, the residents themselves varied as much as the property types, gardens, and locations. We saw everything from meticulously manicured front lawns with neat hedges, newly painted front doors, and sweetly tuned doorbells, to varying degrees of assault courses with overgrown weeds and nettles, leading to neglected and shabby front doors with no bells or knockers. I sometimes dreaded the door being opened!

One of the girls in the team was short of money, as I was, and on one occasion she wore a long, faded, striped-cotton skirt. It reminded me of a bed sheet, but I wasn't going to mention it. However, it seemed I didn't have to, because she proudly announced that she had made the skirt herself from an old sheet. "Really!" I said, trying to sound as surprised as possible, but I didn't get to see the full extent of her handiwork, because as she made her way up one of the unkempt gardens, her flowing skirt became snagged on a rambling rose bush, and in the poor girl's efforts to yank her skirt back, the fabric ripped clean in half! We both laughed hysterically, but she, sadly, had to call it a night.

Times were tough, but only financially – I loved life and living. Somehow I still managed holidays, because there was still the profit-sharing scheme at work. I used to go abroad with my eldest sister, Ann, and her family. The arrangement generally was that I took my driver's licence and drove the hire vehicle whilst abroad, so we could all enjoy days out with the children. I paid a nominal amount for the accommodation and food, so it worked out very well. We even went back to Barbados and stayed in a lovely villa not far from my aunt and uncle's place, so we got to see them at the same time. We befriended the maid who came to our villa each day, and she asked us over to her place in the hills for tea one day to meet her family and see where she lived. We found the house without too much difficulty and had a really nice time – she was a lovely, genuine lady, who looked to be in her forties.

It was getting dark by the time we left, and in Barbados there isn't much sunset. The sun disappears really quickly, as they are so near the equator, and it goes dark very suddenly. The maid (I can't remember her name) had warned us not to stop for anyone, as there might be thieves around. We left in our little Suzuki people carrier and headed downhill back towards the villa.

As we drove along, a group of youths appeared from out of nowhere and put their hands up for us to stop. Given what we'd just been told, I had no intention of stopping for anyone, not least because we had children with us. Instead I put my foot on the accelerator, beeped the horn, and drove straight through them. Of course, they might have been innocent and friendly, but we'd already had our quota of innocent and friendly for that day.

Overall I remembered this Barbados holiday well because I had such a good time. When we were being driven to the airport for our return transfer, I was actually crying, because I didn't want to go home. How embarrassing that was in front of nephews and nieces – Auntie Nessa is crying because she doesn't want to go home! The children were so well behaved and mature by comparison. I got over it.

Back home, whenever I met with friends, there would always be a story to tell. The time had really flown by since I'd left London four years earlier. But if ever I was faced with a dilemma of any kind, I would find solace on a little bench outside a church in one of the "chocolate box" villages I used to visit. Here I would sit at the top of the hill, feeling a sense of "we shall overcome" and thinking about the dilemma at hand until some sort of divine intervention reduced it to a mere inconvenience that time would sort out (that *time* normally being the end of the month – payday). I think I always went there with the expectation that I would get my problem resolved, so I invariably did.

Finchingfield was a typical country village, with a church on a hill, a couple of village pubs, and a village green next to a duck pond. It was a timeless place, and the small grocery store had probably been there for decades, serving its locals with essential provisions and customary gossip, come rain or shine. The shop itself had probably not changed much. The sign hanging inside was probably more in keeping with current trends, but humorous nonetheless. It read: "God helps those who help themselves – we prosecute!" This always made me smile.

Winter was soon in full force. The snow and ice hadn't shifted in days, and the roads were becoming seas of sludge, not the ideal conditions for riding a motorbike. I felt a bit like an intrepid explorer as I left the flat one morning for work. I was wearing countless layers of warm clothing and gloves, to the point that, by the time I'd stretched my waterproof garments over the top, I could barely walk or move my fingers. The bike was started by an electric button, fortunately, which was a relief, as I don't think I could have bent my knee enough to have kick-started it.

Anyway, slowly and very carefully, I started my 15-mile journey to work. Everything was going fine, but for some strange reason, about 10 miles through the journey, the bike just died. There was no power left at all, so I had to coast to a standstill at the side of the road. Now, this was in the days before mobile phones, and my belonging to a roadside assistance organization was completely out of the question. I could have left the bike and walked to a phone box, but I decided to stick out my thumb to all passing motorists and see what happened.

Unlike the films, it was hardly a case of using my womanly wiles; I was hardly attractive under so many layers of clothing and waterproofs and a crash helmet with the visor closed firmly for that extra bit of warmth. Little wonder that most people carried on driving past! However, one other rider did stop to help, and he actually managed to start my bike again as I stood there like a spare part. Unfortunately he was back on his bike and zooming off again before I had a chance to thank him. But there came another chance, when I saw the same guy on his bike a few weeks later while I was out for a ride one evening. Actually, I was only out for a ride because I wanted to avoid paying the milkman, who was out on his rounds collecting money. I'd seen him walking across the car park at the front of the flats, so I'd nipped out quickly round the back.

I'd just got to the end of my road when this guy went past on his bike. He must have recognized my bike but (hopefully) not me, as I was now out of the full regalia. I set off in hot pursuit. Soon the guy stopped outside a Chinese take-away, so I managed to have a chat with him. I had to pretend I was on my way past, as there was no way I could afford a Chinese take-away.

Anyway I was able to thank him for helping me that fateful morning on the way to work, and I offered to buy him a drink some time. He smiled and agreed, and we met up one lunchtime in a pub near where we both worked.

His name was Dave. He was single, a few years older than me, handsome, hunky, and he lived at the end of my road – *result!* We started dating and got on tremendously well, very much like brother and sister – perhaps too much like brother and sister. We had the benefit of each having our own space but being nearby if we wanted to get together – which actually was quite a lot, but neither of us would admit to the other how we really felt. As a result, our relationship was very much on and off, which was not a good state of affairs.

Unfortunately, it was during one of our "off" stages that I needed Dave most. I came home from work one day to find the front door ajar – I'd been burgled, along with my next-door neighbour. As burglaries go, and given that I had little to steal, it wasn't so much horrendous as extremely unnerving.

I decided it was time to sell up and move on; I'd been there seven years. Obviously, I'd be staying in Essex because of my job, but I fancied living in a house next time. I used to think that flats were safer when you lived alone, but while the burglaries were random, I did take them personally and felt I'd been targeted.

4

Twenty-Seven to Thirty-Six

I moved to Colchester now, because I had some good friends there, and as my finances had improved somewhat, I was also able to enjoy the mass of pubs and bars by night and the extensive shopping centre by day. Friends, pubs, shops – these were my priorities, but I unfortunately lacked the obvious foresight to see that my journey to work would now take even longer and therefore cost more in fuel and time. However, I was trading a flat for a house in a better area, so to me at least, it was a good all-round move.

The house I found was a little Victorian two-up two-down, at the end of a small terrace, which reminded me of one of the pretty houses we had overlooked in the London flat. In this case there were only ten houses on each side of the single-lane street. The back garden was about the same size as the house itself. It was neatly turfed and surrounded by other gardens. Although it was only five minutes' walk from the town centre, it was remarkably quiet.

Within two months of moving in, I had gone through the house like greased lightning and decorated whenever and wherever possible. Although still on a budget, I could afford a few tins of paint and various cleaning products, which can do wonders to any little retreat. The house was clean, fresh, and tidy, and it felt very much like home – my home. Dave helped where he could, as we were now "on" again, and we saw each other at weekends and were getting on better than before.

Travelling to work was initially no problem either, as I had a car-share arrangement going with the guy I had bought the house from and his friend (all above board, and they were both happily married). I just contributed to the fuel each day because they didn't incur parking costs.

It seems that when one thing changes in life, so does something else. The office where I worked had a change-around to a different part of the building. This time my desk looked out onto a road, across which lay a piece of wasteland. One Monday morning, I came in to work and noticed that during the weekend a group of travellers had moved in across the way. I didn't take too much notice, except for the dogs running around – a dark brown-and-white spaniel with two completely brown puppies. They all seemed perfectly happy and playful, and this was a cheerful sight to see each day.

One morning I noticed that there were only half the number of caravans there, and it was obvious that many of the travellers had now moved on and taken the mother dog and one of the puppies with them. I felt sorry for the little puppy left behind – presumably given as a gift to one of the remaining families. However, I soon realized that the puppy wasn't being as well looked after as before. One day, I saw one of the children trying to push this fluffy brown ball into the road – a busy road at that – and I decided to take action. I went across to see the travellers that very lunchtime. After a little negotiation and a lot of smiling on my part, we agreed that I could buy and collect the puppy the following Sunday.

Sure enough, all went according to plan, and Dave and I took the puppy home. She was extremely nervous, but you could see the intelligence in her eyes and the understanding that we were not going to harm her. She was covered in splashes of green paint, and her ears were thick with mud, so we bathed her, fed her, and then watched her sleep for the rest of the afternoon, totally exhausted from her ordeal. She now looked like a fluffy brown bear, so we named her Gypsy Bear Hound. It wasn't just her coat which was soft but her nature, too. She was the gentlest dog I have ever known.

Gypsy was just three months old, and initially she lived in the back garden during the day while I was at work. There was an outhouse (it had been the outside loo and coal shed years ago), so her cosy bed and food bowls fitted very well. She could use this place to keep warm and sleep, yet she was still free to roam the garden if she wished.

Each evening when I got home, she'd come into the house until the next morning, but it was a while before she could quite master the stairs. She could get up them but couldn't fathom how to get down again, so she would bark for me until I came to pick her up like a child and carry her down. Gypsy had truly made my life wonderful, and Winston wasn't too put out either, although I'm sure he didn't feel quite the same way about her.

Gypsy and Winston

Some of the best times I enjoy remembering are those when, on a cold Sunday morning, I'd prepare a casserole to cook slowly in the oven. Dave and I would then take Gyp for a really long walk, stopping at a pub – Guinness for us and crisps for Gyp – before heading home to a lovely hot dinner for all of us in front of a real fire. Then we'd all crash out for the rest of the afternoon and sleep. These simple pleasures are more deeply rooted in my memory than the many holidays abroad which, enjoyable as they were, could be had at any time and didn't represent the good old days.

Gypsy grew to be a fine dog, and with the minimum of training she would do many impressive things, like going to fetch the letters from the front doormat in the mornings, going upstairs to fetch my slippers (although only one at a time), and even searching for my keys and bringing them from places like the upstairs mantelpiece. I'd just tell her what I wanted and where they were, and off she'd go, completely understanding my request. She'd be so pleased with herself when she returned with the goods. When Gypsy's tail wagged, her whole body wagged as a counterbalance!

Sometimes Dave would take her to work with him, and occasionally she came along when we went to fly in Dave's light aircraft – she was always as good as gold.

Dave and I enjoyed each other's company, but we didn't plan a future together. Perhaps this is why the years simply merged quickly into a decade before we knew it. Strangely, I didn't actually *need* anyone, and I don't think Dave did either. I felt a great sense of deep inner peace. My quality time was spent with friends, giving dinner parties, or pottering about the house and garden. Mum and Ken still visited, as did Vicki and Cyril. The house was so near the town centre it made for a great weekend, because we could simply walk into town in minutes for shopping, sightseeing, theatre, cinema, or restaurants.

Weekends on my own were just as good. A typical Saturday would start with taking Gypsy into town for some food shopping. The first stop would be the butchers', Frank and Cyril (another Cyril), who were such good fun and so witty. They served me well, with large steaks and joints of meat at the beginning of the month (after pay day) and then down to sausages and chicken drumsticks towards the end of the month. Regardless of my budget, I always felt like a truly valued customer, and I so enjoyed our small talk on any subject which came to mind.

Next I'd shop in the adjacent greengrocers, and then go down some steps to the little market for a browse and maybe to buy some housey magazines, slightly out of date, before heading back home via the chocolate shop. There were no bargains here, except the wonderful chocolate aroma and exquisite delight of selecting six individual home-made chocolates, such as plain chocolate, rum truffle, and cherry liqueur (well it *was* the weekend!). This would represent a very good Saturday morning. Back home, I'd let Gypsy into the garden with her bones to chomp on, put the shopping away, and help myself to a mug of freshly percolated coffee before sinking into the sofa with my feet up, magazines on lap, and exquisite chocolates at my side – sheer, unadulterated bliss!

Then I'd get inspired by all things housey and spend part of the weekend moving furniture and pictures around. Grass cutting and car washing came as standard every few weeks, and I tended to do these one after the other, so it was very good exercise, and I was out in the fresh air. Dog walking was at the local garrison field, and I felt very safe here, as many other dog walkers and sports people used the field, which was meticulously kept. Gypsy just loved charging around and chasing her ball. At weekends I tended to walk over to the field with Gypsy, but weekdays I drove after work as it was a lot quicker. Gypsy was just as excited either way.

Of course, security was always an issue by virtue of the place being a garrison, and I always carried ID. Sometimes the barrier would be down in the entrance road and soldiers would do spot checks on vehicles, so a few times I had to get out of the car and let them have a good old rummage (the car, not me).

The neighbours were all very friendly and not too nosey. One of the neighbours I met over the garden fence was Win, a lovely lady and a very caring nurse. She was also interesting to talk to. One day she said that she was going to see a medium with her friend, and asked whether I wanted to join them. It would be a trip out, and although it was an expense I could have spared, I decided to go along just for the ride.

After a forty-five-minute drive, we arrived at this guy's house near the coast. Beside the front door was a brass plaque with his name on, and so far I was moderately impressed. Then we entered a waiting room – complete with receptionist – and I realized that this was quite a serious set-up.

My appointment was last. I was feeling quite apprehensive by the time I went in, not least because when Win's friend had come out of the next room, she had been in tears, and Win had had to take her for a walk! The medium was quite a character and full of life and energy. He was using a cassette tape player to record the session for me; I still have the tape. He pointed out on the tape recording that he and I had never met and what he was going to tell me was information he was "receiving". I'd never been so gob-smacked in my life, as this man who was sat before me reeled off my upbringing, parents' personalities, romance and – perhaps most important for me at that time – what the future would hold. In no uncertain terms, he said that I was going to meet a very good man in due course – not immediately – but I would love this man more than anyone else in the world and be treated like a queen. We would marry, and it would be my only marriage, and it would be blissful. "You have a life to behold," he said. "As the spirits are leaving, they are turning and saying, 'Enjoy your life – you have earned it.'"

Not surprisingly, I left that place in tears as well! This future wasn't to happen for a while yet, but whenever I was down, I had the tape to listen to and take heart from.

For the first two years after I moved in, the house next door was empty and really quiet. However, this all changed when some young students moved in. Jackie,

Jo, and John were all okay, actually, but I couldn't believe how the noise travelled through the house when anybody ran upstairs or even had a conversation. Fortunately the "studes" were very good-natured and loved Gypsy to bits.

Jackie, tall and athletic, with long dark hair, was taking French and Spanish. Jo was shorter, blonde, and taking English literature, and she was John's girlfriend. John, with his wild, wiry hair, was studying law. Sometimes the "studes" would take Gypsy with them to the university and take it in turns to dog-sit between lectures within the grounds of the campus. There was always a funny story to be had, like the day she went for a swim in the lake and came out sopping wet, spraying water over everyone as she shook herself! I enjoyed telling people that my dog was very intelligent and went to university; she had also travelled by road, rail, water (ferry), and air!

To assist with her studies, Jackie took some time out in the south of France and became a nanny to the children of a French family for a few months. I knew I'd miss her terribly, as did Jo and John, so after only a matter of weeks, the three of us decided we'd go down and see her for a week. Jackie, bless her, was rushing around finding accommodation for us all while we found the cheapest travel option, which was by coach – or coaches, in fact. Dave was looking after Gypsy and Winston.

The journey seemed to take days, after many stops to change either driver or coach. I'm sure I would have got lost if I'd been alone, as finding the right coach in the dark among about fifty in a car park was not the easiest of tasks, especially when the only thing on my mind was getting to the loo in time rather than what our coach or driver looked like!

When we finally arrived in Nîmes, it was late evening. Although we were very tired, we were pleased to see Jackie waiting. Jo and John were staying in bed-and-breakfast accommodation in town. Jackie took me to a house, where I'd be staying in the flat above. We were met at the large iron gates by a lady who said, "Welcome, Vanessa. Please do come in; I am Mme Duval. Have you had a good journey?" I replied that the journey had been fine and thanked Mme Duval for allowing me to stay. Luckily, she was an English teacher, so I felt immediately at ease, as I do not speak French.

After arranging to meet the next day, Jackie left, and Mme Duval led me to the upstairs flat of her beautiful home. The style inside the flat was typical classic chic, with marble floors, elegant chairs and furnishings, and large, dark wooden bookcases stuffed with probably some excellent reads (if you could read French). Outside there was a tiny balcony on which to sit and relax. But now it was late, and I was tired, so I went straight to bed and to sleep.

In the morning I went to the bathroom and, while running a bath, opened the large windows inwards. I unlatched the heavy wooden shutters which were letting in shafts of sunlight through the slats. The next experience I could only liken to *The Wizard of Oz* film, which starts out in black and white. Dorothy then opens the door and sees a paradise of sunshine and colour come streaming in. Just like Dorothy, I flung the shutters back, and I will never forget the sight before me. As far as the eye could see there was a mass of beautiful flowers, trees, and shrubs, all presented in a massive landscaped garden. I actually said, "Wow!"

Just below the window lay a large stone patio, very wide and stepped. Just to the left of this, glistening in the morning sunlight, was the deep blue water of a rectangular swimming pool. This was amazing, and I felt very humble and privileged. I know that many people have these holidays all the time, but this felt so different, because it was all based upon a few people getting together and showing the extent of their kindness and generosity.

Monsieur Duval was quite shy about the place, as was his daughter – their other daughter was in Vienna and their son in South Africa at that time. Jackie, Jo, and John paid a few visits, and we all enjoyed that luxurious pool. Coupled with the luxury of chocolate croissants, which I had now become addicted to, I was truly in seventh heaven.

To my utter surprise, Monsieur & Mme Duval would not accept any money for my stay. Mme Duval just asked if I'd help her prepare some food for a dinner party – one to which I was also invited! Of course I helped, with pleasure, and before the guests arrived I gave this generous couple a bottle of champagne (something they probably drank all the time, like any other wine), accompanied by a box of chocolates and some pretty flowers. Perhaps a bit cheesy of me, but it was all I could think of.

"Oh you shouldn't have," sighed Mme D, while her husband sat *tutting* and shaking his head. I hoped that I hadn't offended them in any way, as I was as ignorant of French customs as of the language – to my shame.

The evening was a real hoot, with very friendly guests, who included the couple who'd hired Jackie as a nanny. (Unfortunately Jackie wasn't there, for obvious reasons.) Mme Duval was able to control the conversation well, speaking enough French *and* English for us all to keep up. She made the interesting comparison that, like Nîmes, Colchester is a historic Roman town and that Nîmes, too, benefits from being near to coastal resorts (it's an easy drive to places like St. Tropez). "I asked Vanessa earlier where *her* nearest coastal resort is," continued Mme Duval to her eager audience, "and it is called 'Clac-ton'." Then, like an echo around the table, came the word *Clac-ton*, as though to ensure it was being pronounced correctly. Mme Duval turned to me and said, "What is it like at Clac-ton, Vanessa?"

I wanted to giggle, but I managed to say, "Um, well, it's nothing like St. Tropez, because it isn't a large resort with a long sandy beach. But it does have a naturally pebbly beach, and also a pier to walk along, and a funfair." Curiosity now satisfied, the subject was changed. *Phew!*

The next day, Mme Duval took me out in her car to various historic sights, like the Pont du Gard, which is a magnificent Roman aqueduct built from massive square stone slabs. This was a cultural eye-opener, just as the whole experience had been, and I felt very privileged.

When I returned home, I wasted no time in sending the Duvals a package of information and postcards all about Colchester – some were even in French. I also sent a photograph of my humble terraced home and said in a covering letter that if ever they were anywhere near Colchester they were more than welcome to stay with me in return.

It was a great joy, a while later, to receive a reply saying that they were arranging a trip to the Lake District and wanted to see Cambridge en route, so they'd very much appreciate an overnight stay and a daytime tour of Colchester. I was delighted, and I spent days getting the house as lovely and welcoming as possible for their arrival. On the afternoon they were due, I cooked one of my favourite meals: pork chops with a cream, garlic, and herb sauce. M and Mme Duval arrived with luggage – and presents! They seemed to like the house and, in particular, Winston, whom M Duval described as *magnifique*. My big tabby with his big, bad attitude must have looked enormous compared with the dainty little French cats.

In no time we were all sitting around chatting, with glasses of wine. M. D took great delight in playing with the cat by running his fingers along the bottom of the settee and then quickly moving them before

Winston pounced. He thought this was hilarious, but I had visions of his hand being ripped to shreds the moment his timing was slightly out! Thankfully he kept his head and his hand.

The next day was gloomy and spitting with rain – typical, just the sort of weather you don't need for a tour around the town. Still, brollies at the ready, we set off on a sort of circular tour which I hope incorporated most tourist sights – extending to Frank and Cyril's butchers' shop down an old narrow street lined with similar traditional shop fronts. Frank and Cyril came out to say hello, which pleased me, because they had heard all about M and Mme Duval and their visit to the town (and had supplied the pork for our meal). The rain was becoming heavy now, so we walked briskly, but M Duval hung back a little, apparently enjoying himself looking up at listed buildings with their exposed timbers and lattice windows. This area is known as the Dutch Quarter, as Dutch weavers once lived here, and the area itself is very pretty.

A little further nearer home, M Duval called out to us and pointed over to a little shop on the other side of the road, asking, "What is this?" I cringed when I realized that he was referring to the private shop with blacked-out windows. Mme Duval was now also looking at me for an answer.

"Oh … er … it's a sex shop," I replied, and I carried on walking in the hope they would too. No such luck; M Duval was too busy thinking about his next question. "What does it sell, Vanessa?"

"Well, *how* would I know?" I expect he was just teasing me. But so as not to disappoint, I said quietly, "sexual accessories!" To this they both laughed – I'm sure they were playing! Fortunately, he didn't wander into the shop, but if he had, I think the rest of the tour of Colchester would have been quickly forgotten.

The visit had been a success, and this lovely French couple went on their way towards the Lake District with a little more insight under their designer belts. For me it had been a real honour and pleasure.

It was ironic that the students next door had all flown the nest already, and once again the house was empty while the owners tried to sell. Unbeknownst to me in my perfect, quiet life, I was about to get a serious wake-up call.

My new neighbours were a young couple, and they were very different from the laid-back students. Within a few days, heated arguments could be heard blazing through the walls, with every expletive going. I was furious and wanted to go round and hand out a few choice expletives of my own, but I decided that a more diplomatic approach might be best for long-term peace and harmony.

The following evening, while I was in the kitchen getting dinner, I noticed a guy in the garden next door. I hot-footed it outside. Still trying to be casual, I said, "Hi! Are you the new owner?"

"No, I'm just helping with the garden," he replied. (Damn!) "But I'll go and get Jane and Pete if you want."

"Yes, thanks." Another guy came out, looking a bit grumpy, and I felt this wasn't a good time. After all, moving house *is* stressful, and the last thing you want is a nosey neighbour hanging over the fence having a moan – but then an issue should be mentioned, shouldn't it? It's amazing how many thoughts go through the mind in a split second, especially when you're searching for a cop-out!

"Hello, I'm Vanessa. I just wanted to introduce myself as your new neighbour," I lied.

"Oh, right. Well, I'm Pete; my girlfriend, Jane, isn't here right now, and this is my mate, Dan," he said. Dan went into the house. So far so good, and now we had privacy.

"Pete, was it you who was shouting last night?"

"Yes, what of it?"

"Well, I was worried that it might have got out of hand and someone might have got hurt."

"Well, no one did, I can assure you." This was not the best way forward and it didn't feel particularly diplomatic, so I had to go the whole hog. "I'm pleased to hear it Pete, but if ever I feel concerned enough, I will need to call the police, and I just wanted you to know that, because I'm a caring person rather than a nosey person."

We both turned on our heels and went our separate ways.

From then on, I found myself regularly turning a blind eye or a deaf ear to the rows next door, which became a regular occurrence. I decided to visit Abigail in Bahrain – the Abi who used to live next door in London. We had kept in touch all this time and it seemed the most natural thing to do was visit and catch up. So I worked out all my flights, flying to Amsterdam to get the connecting eight-hour flight to Bahrain, and I'm so glad I did. When I arrived at Bahrain Airport, there were many people about but I collected my luggage for my two-week stay and then went in search of Abi, who was collecting me. It dawned on me at that point that we hadn't seen each other in ten years and might not recognize each other, but I didn't panic. I just walked past all the people at the arrivals gate and there she was, as pristine and immaculate as ever.

Dear Abi looked after me so well, having taken two weeks' annual leave from her job as a PA, and she had planned all the places and people we were going to see. She even had a horse (named Calypso), which we wasted no time in seeing. As horses go, he was a bit stroppy with attitude. He was really dark brown in colour – almost black – and quite a handsome beast, although not huge in stature. I rode him, but not for long (my choice rather than his).

One horse I did fall for at the stables was named Dinghaan. He was large, handsome chestnut, with a white blaze on his face, and he had such a wonderful, gentle nature. I really connected with him, and he'd happily rest his velvet-soft muzzle in my hand and let me snuggle into him.

Dinghaan

But now back to reality. I did still keep in touch with Abi, although she moved from country to country. There were a few friends I'd kept in touch with, but not many, and I didn't seem to make many new friends. This was now the mid-1990s, and my boss, who was based in London, asked me to go and work in his team there. Things were turning full circle, as London was the place where I'd started working all those years before. I said I'd think about it.

There seemed to be three hurdles to get over. I would have to do a job that was different to my previous one. I'd have to get on with the people I'd be working with. And I'd have a lengthy train journey each day.

No amount of supposition could replace the attitude of "suck it and see", "kill or cure", "do or die", etc., etc. This new focus could be just what I needed. I said yes, with high hopes, and started the new job in February 1997.

Travelling was not a problem. The trains were mainly reliable and there were plenty of them. I preferred the old slam-door trains, because the seats were really springy and comfortable with underneath vents dishing out plenty of blissful heat on my cold legs. Best of all, though, were the intercity trains, their buffets providing lots of goodies – in particular, the piping-hot bacon baps and hot coffee, which, coupled with a good magazine or book, made me feel as if I were going on a holiday. (Let's face it; *anything* other than sitting in traffic on the A12 was like a holiday!)

At the end of my ten-minute walk from Liverpool Street station stood the tall building where I would be working on the sixth floor. Inside there was an impressive foyer displaying wall-to-wall marble, including the reception desk, which was flanked by a waterfall and masses of jungle-type foliage, which looked real enough. Maybe I *was* on holiday, after all. The staff couldn't have been more welcoming, even though I knew most of them already.

Every effort was made to train me for the job, and I even used my Dictaphone to give myself notes which I could replay later. So all in all, after three months, I decided that this move had been a success, and I felt generally happy with the way things were going. There was even progress on the neighbour front, because Pete had left, and it was peaceful next door again.

The money situation had improved, too, and I was able to indulge myself with regular lunchtime shopping trips within the constraints of high-street stores. Designer labels were completely out of reach, but they have never been particularly important to me.

Keeping slim was also a plus point, thanks to my running up six flights of stairs each morning into the office. It wasn't a deliberate attempt at keeping fit so much as the fact that I deplored lifts and avoided them at all costs, following some unpleasant experiences years before. The first time had been a mere inconvenience – the lift had only stuck for seconds before moving again. The second time had been in the same week and same lift, at the office in Chelmsford. It was a Friday at 5 p.m. when there was a sudden jolt and stop on the way to the ground floor. I pressed the alarm but couldn't hear anything. Then I pressed all the buttons – any floor would do! Still no joy.

The walls of my metal box were starting to close in on me, just like the claustrophobia itself. I could feel nothing but the hot flushing of my cheeks as the panic welled inside me. What if I were here for the weekend?

I thought my heart would jump out of my thumping chest. Suddenly the lift moved, and it stopped at the next floor, although I had to step up to the floor when the doors opened. The whole experience could have lasted only minutes, but at the end of it I was a complete mess. I continued shaking for several minutes afterwards. Avoiding lifts was the only option thereafter. I have since used them, with reluctance, only when there was no other choice.

The only other hang-up in my life was my fear of spiders – not good news when you live alone. There were a few occasions when I had to get neighbours in to deal with the massive ones, because I just couldn't deal with them or even look at them, because they terrified me. I found this very frustrating, but I found a positive when I heard about researchers in Cambridge asking for people with arachnophobia to contact them, which I duly did. There's always a first time to be a guinea pig, so why not? I thought.

The research was about the link between stress and memory. Basically, I had to read and remember as much as possible from some blurb they gave me and then recite it afterwards. Then they brought in some spiders in a glass bowl to show me, and then they asked me to recite the information again – it was now very difficult to do.

I hope I helped them. As far as helping myself, it didn't do the trick, and I continued to be on my guard every autumn for the regular troupe of scary bugs. Strangely, *dislike* wasn't the issue; it was just the fear trigger.

Then I heard about the Friendly Spider Programme at London Zoo, especially for arachnophobes, so I booked myself a place. Off I went in search of this miracle cure (which was not the best attitude, since helping one's self was essential). In fact, I found it really helpful to meet so many people in my situation and learn all about spiders and to see all the various shapes and sizes in the arachnid tanks before the big finale, when you had to actually hold a tarantula. I did it, and I have the Polaroid photo to show for it, with me looking *very* apprehensive! The spider itself was like a furry toy. It didn't move a muscle, which was just as well, as it occurred to me that I might panic and stamp on it without thinking – luckily I didn't!

As I was leaving, a lady and her husband approached me and thanked me. Apparently the sheer look of horror on my face as I held the spider had inspired this lady to be brave too.

When I got home, I didn't go round picking spiders up, as I'd hoped I might – this wasn't a miracle cure – but I did feel so much more confident within myself because I had gone on this course. Because I now felt more confident, I chose to ignore spiders whenever possible, so my quality of life did improve.

We were now in 1997, and I felt great –confident and happy. I still saw Dave some evenings and had many friends who I kept in touch with, mainly by telephone, keeping up to date and feeling quietly assured of our alliance. If there was a proverbial blot on the landscape, it was the next-door neighbours again. More and more people started moving in with Jane, and the slamming doors and shouting started up again, but with different voices this time. It didn't take much to work out that people were taking drugs in there. The pale, gaunt, and unhappy occupants were hardly a good advertisement for the benefits of taking drugs.

I felt angry that I had sacrificed so much to get where I was (not very far perhaps) and then have this

problem right on my doorstep. I felt especially angry
one particular August Bank Holiday weekend. I looked
out of the front window in anticipation of Mum and
Ken's arrival to see a black dustbin bag outside on the
path (there were no front gardens). The bag was from
the next-door neighbour and was so full of beer cans
that it was open at the top. It was getting smelly in the
midday sun and attracting swarms of flies and wasps.
This was actually the result of somebody's attempt to
clear the house up.

I knocked on the door to ask if they'd move it to
the back of the house, where the rubbish is collected.
However, there was no one in, so as a short-term
solution, I thought I'd cover the whole bag with
another black bag to deter the hovering swarms. As
a safeguard against germs as much as anything, I put
on some leather gloves and gently placed the bag over.
Suddenly something pricked my middle finger. I took
off the glove and saw a pinprick of blood caused by a
needle-stick injury.

Before I had a chance to comprehend what was
happening, Mum and Ken had arrived. In no time they
had me in the car, with rubbish bag in boot, heading
for the local refuse tip, where they asked for the bag to
be emptied and photographs taken if necessary.

We looked on silently and shocked at the fifty or
so used needles and syringes lying there pathetically
amongst the varied colours of empty beer cans and
cigarette ends. Photographs were taken as evidence, and
the men at the site also contacted the environmental

health office. This could, after all, have happened to a refuse collector, or even one of the children living in the street.

The next stop was the hospital for a blood test – some weekend this was turning out to be! We had to wait for several hours to be seen. I felt so thankful that Mum and Ken were there and surprised at how good-natured they were about the whole situation. Nothing was too much trouble, just as long as I was okay.

While we were waiting, there came a sudden rush of activity when an unconscious man was rushed through on a trolley, with a woman who was presumably his wife in hot pursuit. In one of the cubicles, shoes shuffled and curtains swished, and then we heard a woman screaming, "No, no! Oh no, noooo!" Word got out (discreetly) that the man had drowned while swimming in the sea and unfortunately could not be saved. It was so very sad and his partner, naturally, was inconsolable. Everyone felt the sadness that day, and a stony silence fell about the place.

After the blood test, we finally went home. I was told I had to wait six months for the results! In the meantime, I would need four anti-hepatitis jabs. It felt really unfair to have lived cleanly in all respects and now to find myself at risk in this way.

When I confronted the strangers next door, they all started blaming each other for the used syringes. The time had come to talk to the rest of neighbours in the street. This resulted in the revelation that the police had been called to our street and the adjoining street more than fifty times in twelve weeks. How could this be? It's true that the area had become rather transient over the past eighteen months, with many of the houses being sold to landlords who then rented them out, but this fact alone should not mean that anyone renting a property or room should be any less responsible or inconsiderate of their neighbours. Whatever the reason, it was as mysterious as the sudden vacating of the house. This was brilliant news, which coincided with the arrival of my test results – I was clear!

I cried tears of relief. Without further ado, I set about selling up and moving on to happier times and places.

5

Thirty-Seven to Thirty-Eight

Events moved very fast and much happened in the next two years. Initially I bought a beautiful eighteenth-century cottage fifteen miles away. The cottage had once been loved, but it had long since been forgotten and neglected – but of course I wouldn't have got it so cheap if it had been more appealing.

At the back of the house, ivy covered one wall and was making its way around the old, small kitchen window. This looked very pretty, but made the room itself very dark. The garden was overgrown and literally knee-deep in ground elder, although it was all clearable with sharp shears, elbow grease, and diligence.

Inside, it was very gloomy and smelt stuffy, but again, this was soon combated with paint, detergent, and plenty of fresh air through the place. There were many large oak beams across the ceiling, which had been painted black, and some had holes and angles specifically carved out while others were curved sideways. Someone said that the beams would have originally come from a ship, as the oak was properly weathered and sound, but I don't know whether that was true. All that concerned me was that they had been adequately treated for anti-infestation and rot. There was one particular beam above the kitchen door which, if I didn't approach it on the right foot, would smack me right on the top of my head – ouch! One morning when this happened I felt physically sick, and my eyes were bloodshot (although that was probably due to lack of sleep), so I saw the doctor for good measure. He said that I was fine and agreed that timber just doesn't give when you hit it. My mind was settled, at least.

I had just two weeks to get the cottage up together – or perhaps I should say shipshape – before I was due back at work. As the ceilings were low, I didn't need a ladder, so the large T-shaped lounge/diner was very easy to put right. There was a huge inglenook fireplace with surrounding brickwork to one wall – this needed no attention. My furniture fitted precisely, as did the pretty pink floral curtains, and with the lovely fresh flowers sent by colleagues, the cottage started to look like a cottage once more.

My decorating was interspersed with massive undertakings of cleaning, of course, and the removal of soiled carpets. It would have made interesting viewing for a TV show – all done on a limited budget.

By the time I'd finished, two of my sisters and a few friends had also visited and were thrilled for me. It had been very productive – moving house alone (except for two removal men), decorating, cleaning, settling in, and starting a new life with Gypsy Dog, who adapted well to all the upheaval. She was adequately compensated by the long riverside walks each evening. Sadly, Winston had died nine months before, from cancer.

It was good to see everyone again when I returned to work. They, too, had been really busy work-wise and had cleared much of my workload, but there still remained a backlog. Nowadays I'd just accept a backlog and clear a little every day until it was all sorted. But then, I felt strongly that I must get everything up to date as quickly as possible. After all, this was a fresh start, and I could now sleep in peace at night.

One of the girls I worked with said one day, "Slow down, Vanessa – you're doing *too* much!" I laughed it off and carried on racing around in my usual manner, still getting up at 5 a.m. so that I could be in work for 8 a.m.

Although I was familiar with many aspects of insurance claims, I was far from completely competent and often referred cases to my boss to ensure that I wasn't making any major cock-ups. Perhaps my rationale would have been stronger had my mind not been racing with negative thoughts like, "I should know this by now. I must be useless and too lazy to learn, and now everyone else is using their own time and effort to help me" etc., etc. These thoughts became louder and louder, my inner critic never letting up. Yet there wasn't any indication at all that anyone was fed up with me or bosses disappointed by my work. The fiction, however, still grew as if it were fact.

In my first week back at work after moving house, my mind was filled with thoughts on getting my work up to date. I wanted everything done and dusted and without compromise, and I wanted it *now*! Of course this couldn't and didn't happen. A serious chain of events had been set in motion.

If any of the events and thoughts I'm mentioning seem familiar, then take heed, and break this routine before it breaks you and the experience haunts your life. Speak to your boss or colleague, talk to your family and friends, and most of all, take time out for leisure and relaxation.

Obviously, the stress of my moving house after dealing with nightmare neighbours contributed considerably to what happened next. During the second week back at work, I developed a strange awareness of my own sitting, breathing, seeing, and living. All my senses were at maximum volume, making these unusual feelings of consciousness very uncomfortable and difficult to keep under wraps. Fortunately, or perhaps unfortunately, I did keep these feelings to myself, so no one was any the wiser to my progressive inner turmoil.

It was 15 August 1998, and the weather was extremely hot. The office was air conditioned, but the trains were not. I had raced to the station after work, as usual, and boarded a train with sliding doors. It was like a sauna – the heat was unbelievable, and that was with the doors still open. I changed carriages in an attempt to improve things, but to no avail, so I resigned myself to the good old-fashioned attitude of "put up and shut up", just like all the other passengers, many of whom had to stand.

By the time the train left the station, the carriage was jam-packed – I'm sure the RSPCA would have something to say if animals were transported this way. Just as we had started the journey, the train stopped. After a wait, and a few glances around at each other, we heard an announcement over the intercom. "We apologize for the delay, ladies and gentlemen, but the track ahead has broken, and we're waiting for further information." We all looked around at each other, and after a few huffs and puffs and a few raised eyebrows, passengers went back to reading their papers or wiping their perspiring faces with handkerchiefs, as the afternoon sun continued to blaze through the windows.

Although not perspiring personally, I was dealing with another type of crisis, with feelings reminiscent of the time when I had been trapped in the lift and the claustrophobia and panic had taken hold. Now I wasn't sure where it would stop – perhaps at the stage of breaking the windows to get out! Luckily, I was suddenly distracted by the crackling of the speaker again and another message, to say that we were just about to move, but that the maximum speed we could travel at was twenty miles per hour. At least we'd be moving, and anything was better than sitting there slowly going mad.

As it turned out, twenty miles per hour on a train is very, very slow, and the temperature was getting very, very high. In an effort to cheer myself up, I decided that when I got off this train, I was going to buy a bottle of red wine and a packet of cigarettes and go home to chill out for the rest of the evening. So, an hour later than expected, I drove my car from the station to the off-licence and then telephoned a friend, Sharon, to see if she'd like to join me. She said, "Sure! See you soon."

Dave turned up just as Sharon arrived, so they both sat, all ears, with a glass of wine while I stupidly relayed, and therefore relived, all the events of my nightmare journey home. On reflection, I should have just said, "I've had a crap day and a crap fortnight; I'm gonna book some time off to rest. I'd love to hear all your news" – but I didn't say or think that at all. Instead, as I wittered on, the conversation piece got lost, and I ended up aggravating my already frayed nerves until I became a blubbering mess of tears and incoherence.

Dave and Sharon were sitting together over on another sofa, and they were looking at each other strangely and making observations like "I've never seen her like this before, have you?" and "Do you think I should have a quick word with her GP?" I knew they meant well, of course, but it felt as if they were alone and I wasn't there at all, which probably was true to an extent. But before I knew it, the call was made to the doctor, who started me on a course of beta blocker-type medication immediately, though only for a few days, and signed me off work sick. Unfortunately, the medication totally disagreed with my system, and I suffered side effects in the form of hallucinations. This was pretty counterproductive, given that my nerves were already in shreds. When you live alone, the last thing you need at night is to see swarms of strange imaginary insects darting across the bedroom. If ever there had been any doubt that I was going bonkers, this was definite confirmation.

I had the sense to stop taking the tablets straight away and see another doctor. This time I was signed off work to rest completely (I hadn't yet gone back, anyway). There were no tablets prescribed, but the general consideration was that I might benefit from alternative therapy like Reiki (the realignment of one's energy throughout the body). I did actually find this very relaxing and helpful. My employers were understandably concerned, and they referred me to a professional counsellor who lived locally, with all costs met by the company. This I also found really helpful, as I could talk with with a complete stranger about such things as where you go from here and be met with a non-judgemental and sincere response.

Friends and family were also supportive, although there were those who scampered away to keep a safe distance for the sake of their own sanity. This I found a bit surprising, as when I was having a weepy session on the phone one day and heard a sigh followed by, "What *are* we going to do with you?"

I tried to carve out a routine where my days were spent making appointments or arrangements to see friends, family, doctor, counsellor, and Reiki therapist. Most visited me, as I didn't want to travel too far. Taking Gypsy for walks was a plus point. Although the beauty of the lovely cottage and garden surrounded me,

I still needed to get out and ease the feelings of panic which would start to grip from time to time throughout the day.

It was impossible to believe at the time – and this is the most important part of this book – but I was eventually to become a better person because of this nightmare scenario, a person with a greater understanding of human nature and suffering. I would learn to recognize my own inner needs and fulfilment, which had nothing to do with success or failure but rather following a path of intuition and of trusting what made me function properly as an individual. This didn't all happen overnight, of course, and it took time and effort to try not to think too much about the uncertain times ahead.

Every day I just made sure that I ate well and did something, like pay a bill, send a card to a friend, bake a cake, or cook a curry while listening to music – whatever I fancied doing, as long as I wasn't overtaxing myself. Then later, I'd watch some TV before going to bed and taking a warm drink. I'd listen to Talk Radio for company until I felt sleepy. Occasionally I would wake up in the still of the night and wait until I heard the sound of a passing car or distant lorry before going back to sleep. I would be strangely comforted by knowing there were other people about.

One night I went to bed to hear faint scampering noises behind the ceiling above me; I thought it must be rats. This didn't bother me too much, but I called in the local council. After going into the loft to inspect the lodgers, they confirmed that it wasn't rats that lived there but bats! Of course, bats are protected, so nothing more could be done, but I didn't mind. This did cause welcome amusement to the family: "It's official, Ness – you've got bats in your belfry!" I did see the funny side, too, and slept better for knowing who my guests were.

I was still confused when I remembered the person I had been – the person who had travelled alone to the Middle East, who had started her adult life alone with a mortgage and in a county where she knew no one, but who had soon found many friends and had felt so happy. Now I had become a shadow of that person. I didn't want to leave the house, and I didn't feel comfortable in my own skin. I might as well have had my soul snatched by aliens! The good news was that that person hadn't gone but had changed, just as the times and lifestyle had done. So my new situation would also change at some point, but it would take time.

Ironically, the previous person and lifestyle were the very factors which had brought about this situation, so I was never going to be the same person with the same lifestyle again. This time I would grow to become a better person, and life was to mean much more to me.

After the first four weeks off work, talking with my bosses on the phone, I decided to attempt to return to the office. This required barrow loads of courage, because I felt I was placing myself in the same position as that which had triggered these events in the first place. I honestly couldn't predict my response to the situation. Acting as normally as possible, I got up early, had breakfast, drove the short journey to the station, and boarded the train (I still had my season ticket). So far so good. It was going well, other than the trembling of my hands. With each stop, I found it harder and harder to continue the journey, until eventually, when it stopped again, I got off. I called my boss and then went over to the return platform to get a train home again. I was probably halfway. I found out it was too soon to return. Of course I was disappointed that I hadn't succeeded, but I had to give it a try.

There was one particular friend who stood out like a bright star, and that was Gill. She came over to see me one day and gave me a great big hug before sitting down next to me, holding my hand, and telling me everything was going to be okay. Gill was a very successful businesswoman, who was married with two grown-up children and spent most of the working week away from home, travelling around the country on her own. As I had been before, she was confident, happy, positive, and great fun. We'd known each other for years and had a good friendship based on mutual respect and like minds. Nevertheless, it still stunned me when she told me how she'd gone through a similar experience, years before. Her children had been young at the time, and she had started to get attacks of panic which had increased to the point where she'd physically collapsed and had to be admitted to hospital.

Fortunately, Gill had benefited immediately from the medication she'd been given and had striven to get her life in order again. Taking control and working hard, she'd managed to carve out a good career and had never looked back. She confessed to be a different person now and so much happier. What an inspiration!

"It will take time, Nessie," she said, "and you will have to work hard at it, but get through this you will, and I'll be here to help you – every step of the way."

Gill was a godsend. On the days I felt seriously wobbly I'd call her, and she'd be over with her overnight bag so that I didn't have to be alone. I owe so much to Gill – not only my recovery but my outlook on life. The work she'd mentioned was hard. I can only compare it to a scenario where your car doesn't start and garages don't exist because this is no ordinary car – it's *your* vehicle to get through life. Yes, there are self-help manuals, but it's your workmanship day in, day out, 24/7, as you try to fathom what the problem could be and how to get going again like before. Others will call and ask how it's coming along. They will even encourage you as much as they can, but at the end of the day, it's you and only you who can sort it out.

Hopes are raised when the engine turns over and starts, so short test runs can be made, though actually trusting the reliability of your handiwork on a journey remains to be seen. I didn't feel confident enough about going back to London again, not just yet.

By late autumn, the views at the back of the cottage were breathtaking. To see the white translucent layers of mist hanging throughout the garden right down towards the tall trees was enchanting, coupled with the reassuring sound of birdsong. I felt my spirits lifting, and this gave me great hope for the future.

While I was out with Gypsy on one such morning, strolling alongside the river, I noticed how slow her steps were becoming and how much energy she was using just for a simple stroll. My thoughts turned to her age, eleven years; that was not especially old for a mixed-breed dog. "Are you feeling all right, Gyp?" I asked, just as I would any other friend. Gypsy looked up at me, and the eyes which usually sparkled with intelligence now seemed filled with despair. I took her straight to the vet, where they told me she had cancer and didn't have long to live. It was very difficult to get my head around the fact that Gypsy, my dearest companion, was going to die. To make matters worse, Gypsy knew this, I'm sure, and took to creeping into my bed at night for comfort cuddles and staying until the morning. I decided that it would be kinder to have her put to sleep, so I made an appointment for two weeks' time. This then allowed me time to invite everyone who knew and loved her (the two went hand in hand, anyway) to come over and say their goodbyes.

I felt very sorry for all the many friends and family who had already been upset *by* me and *for* me and who were now being upset *with* me. The one proviso I asked was that they all bring along biscuits and any other treats for Gyp, who fortunately continued to eat and had been forbidden these goodies by me throughout her life to ensure her teeth and gums stayed healthy. Under the circumstances, it was time for treats and indulgences aplenty.

Apart from Dave, Julie and Phil were gutted by this news, as they too were close to Gypsy and had also looked after her admirably on many weekends when I'd been away. They'd once presented me with a beautifully framed enlarged photograph of Gypsy, taken after a dinner party when she had rested her head at the table to scrounge any leftovers. Naturally she gave her best expression – a combination of urgent need and complete adoration of food. The picture was now to be a very treasured possession.

Dave kindly offered to come to the vet with me on the fateful day and then to bury Gyp in his back garden, a place she knew very well. Two weeks later, we were doing just that. It was a rainy Saturday in October, and Dave, bless him, was digging as the rain trickled down his face. Just as I was wondering how much "rain" was tears, he looked up and breathlessly said, "I'm bloody glad you didn't have an Irish wolfhound!" A smile was just what we needed.

Life was never going to be the same again, yet strangely, it didn't feel any worse. Colleagues from work began to come over and visit me now to offer their comfort and support. People never failed to amaze me. Their visits, although welcome and appreciated, were still not enough to give me that extra push to get back to work. This was becoming a big problem for me. The question was *when* would I be ready? To keep myself occupied, given my interest in interior design, I took a home tutorial course, which I found very enjoyable and could do at leisure without the stress of a target to reach.

If ever I wanted confirmation that there was still a little way to go, it came from a visit by Mum and Ken one weekend. They had noticed from an earlier visit that the kitchen could use another base unit so they had brought one along with them from a DIY store. Unfortunately, it was a flat-pack. One look at the pages of instructions – having found the correct language – with such minute print was enough to send anyone into a panic. I simply had to admit defeat, so poor Ken was left to sort it out in the kitchen while Mum was giving me a pep talk-cum-lecture about picking myself up and getting back on track (an apt cliché indeed).

At this time I found my relationship with Mum very strained, as her patience with me was very limited. As a result, their stay that weekend was very short. I was not upset so much as angry at Mum's clear disappointment in me; I had not expected my mother's love to be so conditional. I remembered the times I'd been there for her and helped her whenever I could – regardless of the situation and without judgement.

By a strange turn of fate, Dad had heard the news, through my sisters, about Gypsy being put to sleep and had started to call me from his home in Kent on a regular basis, because he felt sad for me. I'd never realized how much I had in common with Dad, but he completely understood how I felt, even though he seemed to know nothing about the other scenario. Dad loved animals more than people; he'd made no secret of this fact throughout our upbringing. I remember him saying, "You can trust animals, Nessa, relative to their natural instincts, but we humans are far more difficult to read. In life you will meet many types of people – some have hearts and some have pendulums, so learn to recognize the difference." Dad was usually neither "heavy" nor philosophical, so this was quite some chat I'd had with him.

By December my visits to various professional bodies had petered out. Somehow I instinctively knew that another aspect of my life was also petering out – the prospect of me returning to work in London. Through the grapevine I heard talk of redundancies, and I realized that this was my opportunity to bring the situation to a conclusion once and for all. Although the prospect scared me somewhat, the thought of going from month to month indefinitely on sick leave was even scarier. Despite my boss's assurances that I needed to be 110 per cent sure of this decision before anything would happen with my job, I asked for all the necessary forms which would allow me to proceed with voluntary redundancy.

I completed all the documents and, together with a letter giving one month's notice, I headed for the post box a few yards from the cottage. It was late December, in the middle of the afternoon, not too cold, and there was some welcome hazy sunshine. I practically put my hand in the post box with the package before I let go and heard it fall to the base of that bright red vault. There was no turning back now. But as I walked slowly home, I heard the strangest thing – birds singing. I stopped and listened; there were not many and not loudly, but birds were definitely singing. That was the moment I knew I'd done the right thing. Admittedly this feeling stemmed from instinct rather than logic.

Mum needed a little more convincing. "Why on earth have you done this, dear? How do you think you're going to manage financially? There's your mortgage and bills to pay, and good jobs don't just land in your lap, blah…"

At one point I held the phone away from my ear so that she could get this all out of her system. I knew she loved me and meant well, but I was still tempted to say, "Well actually, Mum, I'm going to sell up and come and live with you and Ken!" I hadn't completely lost my sense of humour. But instead I pacified Mum with assurances that I *had* made the right decision, one which would affect the rest of my life, and she'd just have to trust my judgement on this.

At this time I also felt compelled to bring a little life back into the cottage, so I went along to a cat rescue centre. Once there, I walked past cage after cage of various moggies of all shapes, sizes, colours, and ages, all waiting for a loving home to go to. The very last cage I came to appeared empty, but a label on the door said there were two black cats inside who were very nervous and probably not good with children. I asked more about them and was told that the 7-month-old cats were brother and sister and had been there since being rescued as kittens. They had spent months being nursed back to health and were now well enough to home, but they always hid under boxes and blankets inside the cage.

If ever anyone needed to pull my heartstrings, this was surely the time. After seeing two round balls of black fur zooming around the cage for ten minutes, I left with the poor terrified bundles in a basket in the back of the car.

At the cottage, the cats immediately found sanctuary under the bed in the spare room, so I decided to leave them there and provide all the food and drink they needed on the floor each day and say a few words of comfort before leaving them to it. They always used the dirt box in the corner, and sometimes they came out briefly for a stroke. The day I came up the stairs to see two little heads peering around the door frame, I knew they'd be okay, though they still scampered off under the bed again. There was a window at the bottom of the bed, so I placed a table right in front of it, high enough so that the cats could see out if they climbed onto it from the bed.

It was while I was putting the washing out one day that I looked up and saw two pairs of eyes looking down on me. The green eyes belonging to Mrs Wax, as I called her, and the big, round, gold eyes to Mr Pye. Typically their curiosity got the better of them, and within a few weeks the cats had ventured into the garden when I was outside. Everything was going to be okay, and the cats had a new life at the cottage, where they could come and go as they pleased.

Despite all this charitable and companion-orientated activity going on at home, there still remained the issue of my finding another job. My confidence was returning once more – I had apparently made a few right decisions recently, including my City and Guilds certificate in Interior Design.

Another course I saw as an opportunity towards a job was one advertised in food hygiene. This was a two-day course at a local education centre and not particularly expensive, so I went along and learned about everything from storing, handling, and cooking food to the cleanliness of the kitchen and utensils themselves. I found this personally very interesting as well as educational. I came away not only safe in the knowledge that my dinner parties would be safer but with a certificate allowing me to work with food professionally. This was another string to my bow for pinning down that next job.

Time was important now. I had the redundancy money, but this was about my new life and working and earning once again. It also meant that a new CV was in order, so I typed one up at the library and took several prints for good measure. A covering letter with any job application would prove more difficult under the circumstances, but I'd have to cross that bridge when I came to it.

Throughout January, I scoured the local newspapers for a job, until one day an advertisement caught my attention. It read something like "Sales assistant required for busy outdoor leisure shop." It was local, and there seemed to be no major responsibilities involved, so I applied and felt very pleased to receive a letter a while later requesting me to attend an interview.

"Why are you applying to work here in our shop when you're qualified in the insurance industry?" asked the site owner at the interview. It was a question

I had already asked myself, so I knew the answer. I explained honestly how I had indeed enjoyed a twenty-year career, but that the daily travelling had taken its toll and eventually I had burned out, so I had taken time out to rest and reflect on things. I told him I did not need medication — which was true. I went on to mention the redundancies and said I had seen them as my opportunity to leave. Now feeling ready to work again, I had opted for a simpler lifestyle, where I would benefit time-wise rather than financially.

It didn't take a genius to work out that I'd had a mid-life crisis of some kind, and furthermore, I was sitting here in his office being honest and open about it. Later that day, at home, I was on tenterhooks wondering whether I'd said too much. Maybe in future I should "box clever" if I were to be employed again. Then the phone rang; it was the owner from the leisure shop to say I had got the job and to ask when I could start.

This was excellent news, and I was thrilled at the prospect of working somewhere again, without any of the travelling or responsibilities which I'd known before. I was completely free once more.

Within a few weeks I was at work in the leisure shop. The shop manager was very easy-going, with a good sense of humour, and I knew immediately that there'd be no problems. After he showed me the ropes (literally), I mastered the till and cashing up procedure quickly, and when I wasn't serving customers, I busied myself spring cleaning the place, which helped make the atmosphere very comfortable.

Despite it being winter, there was always something to do. Apart from serving customers, there were telephone orders still coming through, deliveries arriving that needed to be unpacked and priced, stocktaking, and sometimes tea making – none of which I minded at all. In fact, this felt like a holiday camp compared with my last job, and thanks to the nature of the business, the customers were generally happy souls who were typically shopping for an enjoyable trip away.

There was a downside, though. I would have to work weekends and bank holidays, which made it a little difficult when friends visited and stayed overnight. Many a Sunday morning I left my guests to get up, feed themselves, and shut the door behind when they left, but they didn't seem to mind. My days off were Wednesdays and Thursdays, and I largely spent this time as I had before, looking around the local shops and sometimes stopping for a coffee and cake.

A new lifestyle structure was now taking shape, and feelings of panic and desperation had subsided considerably. I learned that a mind can either think positively or negatively at one time – it can't think both together. There were many enjoyable things to think about now, and springtime was just around the corner.

Among my new time-filling repertoire were trips to a little art shop in the town, where they framed original oil or watercolour paintings as well as limited-edition prints. I really liked this shop, because there was something very unpretentious and timeless about it. The chap who ran it always came out from his workshop to greet customers with a cheery smile. It was here that I had bought a medium-sized coloured print of a family of foxes in woodland. This picture was appropriate for my home, as it was framed in black wood and looked great against the mass of black beams in the lounge. It felt instinctive to ask one day if any help might be needed in the picture shop for two half days a week. With a wry smile, Max picked up a sign he was about to place in the shop window asking for a part-time assistant!

This move was orientated more towards therapy than money, so I asked if I could be paid in pictures, as there were a few oil paintings I had my eye on and would probably end up buying anyway. Max was fine about this arrangement and happily removed any requested "pays" to the back of the store.

All I had to do was keep the shop clean, arrange the window display, serve a few customers, and fetch coffee and cakes from the bakers. I had learned a little about picture framing, and I helped Max cut the frames or stretch the oil canvases when required. This was bliss – I enjoyed being there as much as Max enjoyed the company.

One day I offered to paint the shop walls. I felt that the plain magnolia did not do enough justice to the paintings, whereas a deep red would set them off a treat. "Fine, we'll do it; I'll shut the shop to customers for a day. Just tell me what paint to buy," said Max. The following Wednesday, with very little effort, we turned the shop deep crimson, and it looked fantastic! The next day we reopened the shop, with the pictures hung in splendour. This was an achievement, and I felt happy despite the intuition that my future did not lie here.

It may seem strange that I was spending more time at work than before, yet I didn't feel this way at all, because I spent so little time travelling. Now there was even more work on the horizon. A country pub about five miles away needed evening bar staff, so I started working there on Wednesday evenings. This meant I worked mainly at the leisure shop for five days, then at the picture shop on Wednesday and Thursday mornings, and Wednesday night at the pub.

A small ad in the newspaper caught my eye and my imagination: Spanish students who were to work in the area needed homes to stay in while improving their English at the same time. I called the number, and in no time, after the initial consultation and check from the agency concerned (to make sure that neither I nor any of the students were serial killers), I met the first one. Augusti turned up one evening and stayed for several weeks. He was young, tall, and handsome, with an excellent manner and good English, which was fortunate for me. He was only 19, but he was clever, confident, very clean, and organized.

The arrangement was very simple: I provided the accommodation, and Augusti could come and go as he pleased. While no meals were required, I did set out breakfast cereal each morning and cooked four nights a week for both of us. Sometimes we'd eat in the back garden, which was nice, especially if friends were over too. Augusti had a brilliant sense of humour, and it was not unusual for us both to be laughing at the same things, especially articles in the newspaper. One day he said, quite seriously, while holding up a broadsheet newspaper, "Vanessa, I have read that Prince Charles is an alcoholic!"

"Not to my knowledge," I assured him. "Read it out to me." Augusti then went on to read aloud about how Prince Charles, during a recent visit to somewhere or other, had been offered some cherry brandy and had really "fallen for it"!

"See!" said Augusti. "He has fallen over because he is drunk!" When I'd finished explaining the expression, it was time for another laugh – who knows what rumours could have been started if he hadn't been put straight.

Although the local job he'd been given was basic work and salary, Augusti did benefit from the night class he attended to improve his English, and I think his overall experience of living and working in England, albeit only for a number of weeks, was very positive and worthwhile for him – and it was very enjoyable for me, too.

The next guy who came to stay was a different person entirely. Raphael was older and shyer than Augusti, and his English was not as good. Within weeks of his arrival, the cottage had a strange smell about it – reminiscent of those circular crystallized deodorant things that used to hang over the sides of toilet bowls. (Well, they did in our house in the 1960s, anyway.) I decided that if we were to continue with this arrangement, he'd have to bin the source of the smell.

Communication wasn't so difficult after I held my nose a few times and frowned. "Ah," he said as the penny dropped. He hastily disappeared, to return a few moments later from his room with a few innocent-looking crystallized balls the size of small marbles.

"I'm sorry, but I don't like the smell," I said. "Can I put them in the bin?" He nodded and then showed me where there were more in his room – in the wardrobe and every drawer! I think they must have been some kind of insect repellent, but en masse and over a period of time, I'm sure they had the capacity to erode away one's sense of smell entirely!

Things didn't improve very much. I found my new guest spent the little time he was at the cottage in his room, and much as I respected his privacy, I found myself wondering what he was doing in there and whether he was okay when he was out. It even occurred to me that he might dislike me or the smell of the old cottage! One such evening, during Raphael's absence, the guy who ran this organization phoned me to ask if everything was still going okay, and I reluctantly told him that I wasn't entirely comfortable and that I didn't think Raphael was, either. "I can do a simple swap with another student," he said without hesitation. "Just give me a couple of days, and this will be sorted."

True to his word, out went Raphael and in came Xavier, who was younger than Raphael, spoke much better English and, just like Augusti, was very polite and smart.

It might have seemed a little optimistic, or even daft of me, but now the cats were settled I decided to get another dog – one which was used to cats and people. I contacted the local dog warden and, surprisingly enough, she knew of a three-year-old bitch which had had four homes already; she needed one-to-one attention and yet was good with other pets. Without further ado, I went to see the dog, Rosie, a Border collie cross. The first thing I noticed was how skinny she was and how determined she was to get on my lap! I "borrowed" Rosie for a day to see how we'd get on. After a few walks and a trip in the car to show her the cats and cottage, I knew this was another hit, so Rosie came to live with us as well. And it did feel good to have a dog about the place again.

Once again, relative equilibrium returned to my lifestyle. I had my local jobs to go to, which were varied and not taxing, a lovely home in a good area, an agreeable lodger (who Rosie adored, playing at his feet all the time), faithful friends who'd stayed in touch, and my family, who were understandably less troubled by my antics these days. Things were indeed looking up. Although I didn't have a special man in my life, I did have a few male friends who I saw occasionally.

One evening when I came in, Xavi said I'd had a few calls and showed me a piece of paper with the names of the callers he'd taken: Jonathan, Kevin, and Chris. I said, "Oh, thanks Xavi; that's really kind of you to take my calls."

He replied, "No problem, Vanessa." Then he continued.

"I have met a few English girls since I have been here, so can you tell me what I must say or do to get English girls to go out with me, please?"

I gave it a little thought and said, "Well, you could say that you're Ricky Martin's cousin!" We both laughed at this. In fact, Xavi didn't have any problem with the girls – English or otherwise – and I did enjoy taking phone messages for him as time went by. I wasn't surprised, as he was not only lovely looking and a sharp dresser but a thoroughly good, kind, genuine person and excellent company.

I felt sad when the summer was almost over and Xavi was to return to Barcelona, but I knew we'd stay in touch as friends. This was also a time for me to have another life overhaul and decide which direction to go from here, as I knew that I would not be a landlady again. Much as I'd enjoyed it, this was not my vocation, any more than was working at three different places each week.

There was now bad news which I had to come to terms with – Dad had died after a very long battle with cancer. This hit the family very hard. If ever we all needed to be united to comfort each other, it was now, but instead we all closed ranks and dealt with our grief in our own private ways. On the day of the funeral, I heard on the radio that there was a nine-mile tailback of traffic on the M25 – my worst nightmare. I knew I just wouldn't get there on time. I called my sister Ann and left a message on her phone explaining that I wouldn't be able to get there. I told her I would go to the church in Finchingfield instead and would think of everybody at 1 p.m. when the funeral was due to start. I felt tearful as I hung up, but just then it rang. It was my friend Win, who used to live near me in Colchester. "Look, Nessa, why don't I come to Finchingfield with you today? You should have someone with you," she said. So I collected my beautiful flowers from the florist and was on my way to the old church in Finchingfield with Win, to the place of comfort where I used to sit and ponder all those years before. Just as we walked through the gates of the churchyard, the grand old clock struck one o'clock. I entered the church as Win waited outside. I placed the bunch of blue irises at the altar and knelt in respect in this empty church. This spiritual closeness, even without a specific religious faith, was just what I needed.

Back at the cottage, I searched for anything that Dad had given to me or made for me – anything from tiny plastic farmyard toys to a chest of drawers. There was a little stool which used to live in the corner of our family kitchen back home; it wasn't particularly attractive, just a hardwood square with legs – but it was a strong and practical piece of handiwork, just like everything Dad had made. It had had various knocks and chips over the years, which revealed all the various layers of paint colours. Now it stood in my under-stairs cupboard, looking as sad as I felt, so I got some black paint and took it into the garden one sunny morning to paint it, with a view to using it somewhere – anywhere but in a cupboard.

Now a very strange thing happened. I was aware that a few gardens away some builders were tending a roof. One of them was whistling a tune, a country and western tune I hadn't heard for a very long time. It was Dad's favourite song by Billy Jo Spears – Blanket On The Ground. This was too uncanny to ignore, and I took it as a sign that Dad wasn't far away at all, particularly since at that very moment I had been painting his own piece of handiwork. It was strange, but I felt closer to Dad in my grief than I had while he'd been alive, and I took great comfort from this.

There were more uncanny occasions like this, including one the following Father's Day, which I'll mention later on.

So here I was, in August 2000, and I had no idea which direction life would take next. Let's face it, no matter how surely you feel you are steering your way through life, there will always be the unforeseen hindrances or strong gut feelings which serve to put the kibosh on everything.

Even if I had been firmly in the driving seat to steer my way ahead, I couldn't have ignored the strong sense of needing to sell the cottage and move on. I felt it so strongly that I got an estate agent round to value the place. After looking around, he said he had a couple who were looking for such a cottage in the area right now, and he wondered whether he could get them round for a viewing straight away.

The next evening, a friendly young couple came round. They hadn't even seen any details, as the agent hadn't prepared them yet, but it didn't matter, because they fell in love with the place and put an offer in the following day for the full asking price. I'm sure we all felt that we had a good deal; the value had almost doubled in two years, so I knew I'd find somewhere else I could afford, and my buyers had their mortgage already in place and were ready to go ahead with the purchase. I can't believe how at ease I felt about the whole thing – considering I had nowhere to go. I had to pull my finger out to start seriously looking. I didn't even know whether I'd stay in the area, but what I did know for sure was that this was exactly the right thing to do, and everything would work out well, and *that's* why I felt so at ease.

For years I'd listened only to my mind and determination, and look where that gotten me in the end. Now I was all ears where my heart and instincts were concerned.

Bear in mind that I didn't have a computer at home. I relied on estate agents' advertisements, local newspapers, and keeping my eyes peeled to see what was for sale in the local area. Sure enough, within a few weeks I saw an old-fashioned semi-detached house come up for sale at the other end of the street. I went straight round to take a look, put an offer in and – bingo – was now buying this two-up two-down late Victorian semi with high ceilings and a massive two hundred-foot back garden. What's more, it was empty, so the purchase would be quite soon, with any luck, and tied into the sale of the cottage.

Pye and Wax

Fox Cottage

6

Thirty-Nine to Fifty-Two

One Sunday morning, I was out walking with Rosie and had my mobile phone with me, in case an estate agent rang about my sale or purchase, which had been moving along nicely. Well, my phone did ring, but it wasn't an agent. It was my friend Win, whose parties I used to go to years before in Colchester, and who had joined me on the day of Dad's funeral.

"Listen, Nessa," she said with some urgency. "I've got Tony round here; he's just popped in to say hello, and he's not seeing anyone at the moment. I thought it would be nice if you two went out for a drink sometime, just as friends. Is it okay if I give him your phone number?"

I replied, "Well, of course it is, Win; that's fine. Thanks for thinking of me. Bye, then."

I was surprised but not worried; Tony was a very safe guy to know. We had a similar outlook on life and we used to talk to each other at Win's parties.

Sometimes Tony would walk me home afterwards, in the interests of my safety. There was never anything in it, as we were both usually with other partners. I always felt protected on those walks home, as Tony was very tall and broad, but this was the only intimidating thing about him. He was the proverbial gentle giant, with short dark hair and soft brown eyes. With his kind, jolly nature and being in my age group, he would be the perfect drinking companion – we had much to catch up on.

I remember very well the evening when Tony phoned. Julie and Phil were over, and as it was such a lovely sunny Wednesday evening, we were out in the garden having a few drinks. I was just talking about the lack of men in my life – or should I say *serious* men in my life – when the phone rang, and it was Tony. He asked if I were free that evening, but as I wasn't, we decided to talk on the phone on Thursday instead. When I returned to the garden and told Julie, she said, "Hang on, Vanessa – you said there were no men in your life, but you've already mentioned three this evening, and now Tony rings you! What's going on?"

We all laughed. It must have seemed strange, but the others were mostly past acquaintances, and Tony was someone I considered to be a good friend.

"We look forward to seeing you again soon," Julie said as they prepared to leave.

"Take care, Vanessa," said Phil. We hugged goodbye, and they left. Who could ask for more beautiful, perfect friends? They were such good fun and so good-natured, with a clever wit, and always immaculately dressed. They had always taken an interest in my life, probably because Julie had been one of the first friends I'd found in the office when I first moved to Essex. She had stayed a true friend and confidante for what was now getting on to twenty years. She was undeniably a special person, with a unique insight and intelligence I have never known before. I felt blessed to have her in my life.

The next evening, Tony rang. After a short chat, in which we established that both of us were at a loose end, he drove over to see me. Once again the sun shone, and it was a pleasant evening. I wasn't at all nervous, and when he arrived we got a glass of cold beer each and went for a wander in the garden. As we chatted easily, it was so obvious that we weren't looking to impress each other or play mind games but just have a pleasant time in the warm evening sunshine. Easy company, that was Tony, and we agreed to meet up again over the weekend. Before we knew it, we were seeing each other every single night!

Win phoned one day and said, "Nessa, what have you done to Tony? He's smitten!"

I just laughed and said, "So am I, Win – so am I!"

Never before had I felt such ease and comfort in anyone's company. It was probably just as well that Tony had to go away for a week on a previously planned holiday abroad with a mate; otherwise, he might have ended up never going home again! As it turned out, we were constantly texting each other throughout his holiday in anticipation of seeing each other again. This was definitely love.

For the last month or so, I had had a large bottle of champagne in the fridge, which I'd won in a raffle at the leisure shop, and I knew that Tony's homecoming would be the perfect time to pop the cork and celebrate. That is exactly what we did. It was fantastic to kiss and hold him again, and we knew this was the real deal. A few weeks later, as we sat in front of the fire, he asked me to marry him. Of course I said yes through a beaming smile. When the contracts were exchanged on the house, we moved in together. It was October, and Tony had a house to sell in Colchester, which he put straight on the market.

It was now heading towards Christmas, my 40th Birthday, and our wedding day – the date we chose was 20 January 2001 We had arranged everything together since October, from renting the venues to getting the invitations printed and sent. Of course we were all set and sorted for our special day.

There was a sprinkling of snow on that bitterly cold day, and Gill and her husband Peter were witnesses at the register office ceremony. The white-frosted trees were the perfect backdrop to our wedding photos outside, because Tony and I wore dark velvet outfits, and the flowers we chose were red and orange roses. The whole wedding party followed our car to the church blessing in Finchingfield. The church that had shared so many of my personal trials of life was now sharing this happiest of days. Then we all went over the road to the pub for our seated lunch in a private room with log fire before going on to a hotel for the evening celebration (many guests had booked to stay the night). A few people had been unable to make it, for various reasons, such as the fog and ice, and I was particularly upset about Phil and Julie. Both had been ill for weeks with flu, and Julie had not recovered enough to come, but I did manage to speak with her at length on the phone a few days before the ceremony.

Tony had arranged our honeymoon – a week in Paris! Bearing in mind that I hadn't even travelled on a train for a year, let alone an aeroplane, I was very nervous about the trip. Mum and Ken were staying at our house to look after the pets, so that was sorted, and Tony reassured me that he would hold my hand all the way. The flight was only about forty-five minutes. Feeling "loved up" definitely helped during the flight – that and the delicious chocolate cake that was brought around with the tea! It's just as well I was chilled, because we were met at the airport by the chauffeur for the hotel and had to use the lift to get out of the airport. Again, this did not present a problem, although I hadn't been in a lift in the years since I'd got stuck in one. Still, life was about *us* now, not just *me*.

We had a brilliant time and the weather was gorgeous for the time of year. We even sailed on a boat down the Seine in the open air and took in many new sights. I'd been to Paris several times before, but it had never looked this beautiful to me. Rose-tinted glasses maybe – I did have much more appreciation for everything now!

The hotel was really plush, and the breakfasts were brought into our suite on a trolley with a silver dome on each plate. The previous night we had selected almost everything on the menu card which we'd placed on the door handle outside – a habit we carry on to this day with some amusement – and so everything appeared the next day: yoghurt, fruit juice, toast, eggs, croissants, jam, cheese, ham, etc. It sounds very greedy, and of course we would have to pay for it, but we have always found that hearty breakfasts like these mean we don't need to stop for lunch, so we get on with enjoying the day until the evening meal comes.

It felt wonderful to be married to such a good and easy-going man. I had developed the habit of using my left hand as much as possible so that I could look again at the ring on my finger and enjoy the butterflies flitting around my stomach. True to his word, Tony had taken good care of me, and we were soon on our way back to the airport for our homeward journey and a new life together.

Back home, there was an eerie silence – I don't mean no traffic or birdsong, but the phone didn't ring, and no one seemed to be getting in touch. It occurred to me that everyone just wanted to leave us in peace. I was about to call Julie to see if she was well again after her flu, but before I had the chance, Phil called and asked me if he could speak to Tony.

I just knew something was badly wrong. As Tony took the call, I sank into the chair with a horrible feeling of dread. Quietly and gently, Tony put the phone down and turned to me. "I'm so sorry, darling, but Julie has passed away," he said. Before he could say any more, we were hanging on to each other in floods of tears. Julie, my beautiful, perfect friend, had been taken to hospital on the day of our wedding and slipped away the following day, 21 January 2001. It seemed she had died from fluid on her brain. Now all her family and friends had a gaping hole in their lives where Julie had featured, and it would stay forever.

How on earth Phil had the strength to cope is still beyond me. He had even made sure that no one told us before, during, or after our honeymoon. I shall always remember his completely selfless consideration in the face of this utterly devastating news. And if we should ever consider the death of a loved one difficult to cope with – we then have the funeral to arrange and deal with.

Phil once again showed his amazing strength and courage – he just got on with everything that needed to be done for Julie's funeral. Of course, he had the support of his Dad and Julie's family, but it must have been an unbearable situation, especially when some of us were so openly in bits over what had happened. I had saved my wedding flowers for Julie, but not for her grave – yet that was where they ended up. This wasn't how it was meant to be for such a bright and beautiful 36-year-old.

We saw Phil several times over the next few months. He was still sane, had lost weight, and had made a decision to go on an organized expedition to Peru for six months to try to get his head together from a distance. When he returned, our times together became fewer and fewer, and I think that had more to do with me than him, because now all we had to share were memories of Julie and her graveside. I felt guilty, because Phil had meant the world to Julie, and she would have been happy for me to look out for him, yet every time I saw him, it was like looking at one half of the partnership – with the other half gone. It was so very sad.

Tony coped well, considering we were just starting out as man and wife. I'd always known he was a gentleman, and now he was proving to be a pillar of strength and understanding as well. It didn't alter the fact that our new life together was going ahead very slowly and quietly, as we adjusted to this lifestyle. We both loved home-making, and we had the perfect place to start. Our house had been in the same family for over fifty years, so it needed a lot of modernization. We didn't even have a fitted kitchen, so there was much to do. Fortunately, Tony's practical knowledge and DIY skills saved us quite a bit of money, where decorating and new floorboards and carpet laying were concerned.

We didn't have much money – Tony had paid for the wedding with the money from the sale of his house, and although our mortgage was low, we didn't earn much between us, because Tony worked at a local electronics company and I worked in the leisure shop. But we knew we'd manage somehow. As it turned out, our early spurts of enthusiasm were a waste of time, because no sooner had we decorated the whole house (which took a couple of years) than we wanted to make it look even better, so we started redecorating again with new carpets and so on. Fortunately our finances had improved, as we both were working for new organizations – Tony as a Risk Assessor and myself as a Business Support Officer. This all happened very quickly, and once again it seemed indicative that some things are meant to be and some things are inexplicable – like the Father's Day when we thought we'd go for a pub lunch in memory of my dad. I got into the car and lifted the locking knob of the passenger door to let Tony in. The knob lifted, but Tony couldn't open the door – it just wouldn't budge. I wound the window down so Tony could attempt it from his angle, but still no joy. In the end, the only way our pub lunch was going to go ahead would be for Tony to travel in the back seat. There was no trouble opening the back door, so we went to the pub with Tony in the back. We had a nice Sunday roast and raised our glasses in memory of Dad.

Not surprisingly, the front passenger door of the car still wouldn't open when we left the pub for the journey home, so once again Tony found himself travelling in the back seat. I joked that it must be Dad's fault, because he wanted to travel in the front seat, and somehow this sort of made sense to me. Tony, on the other hand, was not so easily convinced; he said he'd phone the garage the next day to get them to sort the door out.

Anyway, the next morning, the Monday, I got ready for work, kissed Tony goodbye, and left the house. I got into the car and wondered whether the door would work. I lifted the button, pulled the lever – and it opened. I then tried it from the outside, and again it opened. I went in and got Tony to take a look – there was nothing wrong with the door. We never had a problem before or after that Father's Day trip to the pub, and I'm sure it was to do with my dad, who wanted to sit at the front. He was, after all, a very proud man.

After marriage, some people might have put their efforts into deciding whether to have children or not, but Tony and I took the view that if it happened, it happened. One day the decision was made for us. I needed to see the doctor one morning. Like me, he thought I might be having a miscarriage, but it turned out that I had internal problems and needed a hysterectomy.

While I was in the hospital, a man walked up to me with a huge bunch of flowers and a box of chocolates. I thought he had come to the wrong bed, but he was a delivery man, and the flowers and chocolates were from people at work, together with a massive card with all their loving best wishes. I was so touched, and it did my self-esteem the world of good. Another aspect I'll remember is that on the day I was due to leave hospital, a nurse came around in the morning to see me with some paperwork, after which, she said, I could get ready to go – which I did. It was great to get ready and put make-up on and look half decent again. I was waiting on my bed for Tony when the same nurse came back in with her clipboard. She took one look at me, frowned, looked around and then back at me, and said, "Sorry, I didn't recognize you!" I laughed – it made my day. She obviously meant I had scrubbed up well!

But this was a difficult time for both of us. After the operation, poor Tony was doing all the running around, shopping, and looking after me for eight weeks. All I could do was mooch around the house until I got my stamina back. I'd heard rumours that after this type of operation you shouldn't even lift a kettle, and it's true – I'd just look at the kettle (full or not) and think, "I can't lift that." I started to worry whether I'd ever be strong again, but of course the body is a wonderful thing, and in time I became stronger and stronger. I was back at work within eight weeks, and other than a few twinges of pain from the scar tissue within, I felt absolutely fine and so glad to be back at work among so many great people.

Besides the superficial feel-good factor that this situation was all over, there was the obvious reality that we were never going to have children. The prospect of adoption didn't really appeal to us. The door was truly closed – we accepted that this was not meant to be and got on with building our mini-empire of a decent home and lifestyle.

Although we didn't intend to live in our house forever, we didn't know how long it would be or where else we would live. It was very convenient for both of us to get to work. There were also so many good dog walks right on our doorstep. One of my favourites was along the field opposite our house, to a very old woodland with oak and holly trees, with twisted brambles just like my childhood days of dog walking. Tony, Rosie, and I tended to go on this walk on a Sunday morning and take a pocket full of carrots and apples for some horses we saw in a field nearby on the way back. The whole route probably took about an hour and a half; the woods weren't too big – otherwise I might have felt uncomfortable with the prospect of getting lost.

It always felt lovely when we came home, left our wellies at the front door, and put the little gas fire on in the lounge – one of the Victorian reproduction coal-effect jobs flanked with coloured tiles depicting irises in a pot. It was both effective and efficient. Overall, the house was lovely and cosy, and Tony had done a fantastic job with his DIY skills. The only thing that continued to bother us was the constant traffic noise day and night, despite the new double-glazed windows. No matter how much we re-jigged the living spaces, there always came the noise of traffic, so our priorities changed, and moving house become paramount. Had we not lived there for six years we might not have been any the wiser, but we knew it had become noisier and noisier and wasn't going to improve, and we now wanted quiet.

We didn't know where we'd move to or when, but as we weren't in a position to give our jobs up, the house would need to be relatively near to where we worked. On a fact-finding mission, we searched the Internet whenever we could, looking for a detached property, preferably semi-rural. The budget was still going to be tight, so every time we saw a house which looked promising, we'd find out exactly where it was and do a drive-by. This turned out to be a good strategy, as we came across all sorts of renovation projects which were far too ambitious for our pockets. For those which did look half decent, we made an appointment to view, only to often be disappointed once we'd got through the front door – not because our expectations were too high but our budget was too low for what we wanted.

Then, one day in January, we found a detached house in a village about twenty miles from our work. The house passed our drive-by test for appearance and peace. It was in a quiet cul-de-sac and had an air of quirkiness about it. Standing tall in the shape of a witch's hat, behind a mishmash of hedge and foliage, the house was clearly in need of some TLC, but not to any great extent so far as we could see. Definitely new windows and doors were required – the aluminium version had long since been fitted, for a start – and the pink render had faded considerably over the years and was now peppered with cracks and patches of repair.

We made an appointment to view one Saturday morning. The inside was light and airy in some parts – such as the front lounge, which was a decent size and square. There was a low brick fireplace which had been a recent addition; it was okay, as were the wallpaper and carpet. The best feature was the high ceiling throughout the house, which gave a great sense of space. The house had been built in the 1930s and had loads of cupboard space and a large, high loft. All the upstairs rooms had part of a roof line showing through on one side of the ceiling where the roof-line ran sideways on. This made these rooms interesting, to say the least, and a nightmare for placing furniture.

Back downstairs was a galley kitchen which ran along one side of the house; it was very basic and in desperate need of upgrading. On the other side of the house ran two reception rooms, one behind the other. Both were quite dark due to trees outside which blocked the light. We both mentioned how much better the rooms would look if the two were knocked through to form one.

Finally, a large conservatory ran the width of the house at the back and overlooked a magical garden, massively overgrown with fruit trees and bushes, with a small pond at one end, surrounded by foliage, which looked as if it had been there forever. Yes, the garden needed a bit of work too.

We both agreed that we could see ourselves living there quite happily, but whether we could afford to do so would be another matter, as our mortgage would be at the very limit of our joint earnings. Other factors to consider included the extra travelling time to work – not too excessive in terms of time itself, but the extra fuel costs and wear and tear on the car would all add up. But we could settle there without needing to do too much to the house, it would be marvellous, and it would be the first house we could really call home, as we'd chosen it together.

After the usual toing and froing associated with house buying, we finally moved in during June 2007.

It was a very long and stressful day for both of us, and I found myself talking to Tony in a sort of Dalek (a mutant extraterrestrial) voice in the end when he asked where I'd put something. I replied "It – is – hanging – up – in – the – cupboard. By – the – back – door." It seemed to be a way of coping with the stress by deliberately slowing down speech!

Luckily I was human again by the next morning, and we had breakfast on the patio. It was lovely and quiet in the truly beautiful, sunny garden, and it felt as though we were on holiday. The animals seemed no worse for wear, although I kept calling the cats every so often in case they ventured too far. Romie, our white rabbit, already had his familiar hutch and makeshift run under a large apple tree. Rosie had us, so she was quite happy. We thought the garden was quite secure, until the next-door neighbour came round and said that our dog was in her back garden, and she would like us to get her back, because she had a phobia about dogs. I apologized profusely, and we called Rosie back and blocked the gap in the wooden fence as best we could in the short term. This was obviously not the best way to become introduced to your new neighbours, and I did reflect on it a bit. Either the neighbour was bonding with me by admitting she had a dog phobia, or she was mentioning the phobia to make us feel worse! We decided to keep a low profile, which happens to suit us best, anyway.

Since we had already spent weeks thinking about where all the furniture would go, it took little time to get straight, and the unpacking was a relatively straightforward process. We'd booked two weeks off work, so no pressure there, and overall it felt very exciting. I just love home-making, and the thought of getting stuck in, with a dogged determination to make this our forever home, was a real thrill. There wasn't anything that didn't fit or look right, except the massive wooden triple wardrobe, which would only fit along one wall upstairs, so we had a sort of dressing room until we got some proper fitted wardrobes and cupboards sorted out. The cliché "getting your house in order" is true in the literal sense, because to get straight and organized with everything around you also reflects on getting everything straight *inside* you. I find I can achieve a great sense of calm and peace in the world by simply having privacy in my home and a place for everything.

After the multitude of repair, replacement, and cleaning jobs, everything started to go well with the house, the jobs, and the lifestyle. We didn't do much socializing and didn't have many friends, but this suited us in our utopian bubble.

The one thing I had learned about friendship is that if you didn't get the balance right you could use or be used. This may sound harsh, but having read somewhere that we can become like the people we spend our time with, it all started to make sense. There wasn't anyone I felt inspired to be like (except Julie, who was a beautiful, perfect friend) or who I found interesting, so I was more than happy with marital bliss – we were two different characters but with the same values, goals, and appreciation of each other in our lives. The few friends we did see enhanced our lives with their companionship and honesty.

These friends and family enjoyed seeing our new home, and Mum and Ken came over to stay very early on. It was lovely to see them, and we so enjoyed being with them. Tony and I had to go to work during their stay, but we'd shown them around the nearby shops, given them a key, and basically left them to it.

When I phoned at midday, Mum was very excited and said they'd had a lovely morning and done a bit of shopping in the supermarket.

"Shopping in the supermarket?" I was surprised, since we had loads of food indoors.

"Yes, dear," she said. "We got some big tins of sweets, and more wine, and got them all home with no trouble – and we're popping out later to take the trolley back." They had wheeled the trolley back to the house! Talk about show you up, but bless them, the stuff they'd bought was actually for us. These sorts of memories are priceless when it comes to remembering our loved ones.

We did see Mum and Ken as often as possible. Their last visit was in autumn 2007. We had a great time, and the weather was still good enough for a barbecue. But that October at their home, everything changed. Mum had a stroke and spent the next two months in hospital, apparently only vaguely aware of what had happened to her. She couldn't speak but tried to communicate, bless her – it was really heartbreaking for all of us. The worst news came – she had passed away. She was 83 years of age and still too young to die; life had still fulfilled her. In many other respects she had been healthy, but as usual, she had overdone it. Not surprisingly, she had suffered her stroke whilst cleaning the kitchen one evening.

It was such a sad time, and we felt so helpless towards Ken and comforting him in his grief. This was not helped by the fact that we didn't live nearby, although he did have the support of his daughters and their families, who lived not too far away. I was able to recall some of her life and times at her funeral. (Well, I say I was able, but actually, on the day of Mum's funeral, I wasn't at all together, and I mumbled my way through the words whilst trying to control my mouth from drooping.) I'd like to share with you what I said (but skip this if you want – although I think I've already mentioned most of it).

> Thirty years ago Mum and I moved into a lovely flat in London (at Crystal Palace). Although it was a bit bland, having just been built, Mum soon got on with choosing colour schemes, furniture, and fabrics, and the flat became a cosy home in no time. Mum really was an excellent home-maker, and she enjoyed pottering about the place and cooking delicious meals and sweet cakes. At weekends, we'd sit in the communal garden with some

neighbours and have a chat and a giggle over cups of tea and home-made cake.

Despite this regular occurrence, Mum never seemed to put on any weight – she was proud of her appearance and looked after herself well in this respect. When we were children, and Mum took us out, she'd make us walk ahead of her so that she could inspect us for any bits of cotton hanging down from our clothes – then, if necessary, we'd get called back so she could remove any offending strands.

Knitting was something else Mum took seriously, and one day I came home from work and found her busy knitting clothes for Romanian orphans, whom she'd seen on TV. She referred to the children as "poor little mites". Her compassion and kindness to those in need was always there and she'd take direct action to help.

While living in London, Mum's social life included church activities and tea dances – once again the lure of cakes may have beckoned! Mum loved to dance and have fun because she was young at heart with a lively spirit. I remember a type of Trivial Pursuit board game at a friend's house once and Mum not only knew the answers to her own questions but everyone else's too!

It was very funny but it didn't alter the fact that Mum was a very knowledgeable lady.

Her faith in God never wavered, despite her many trials in life. It's fair to say that it was her faith which gave her the immense strength and courage to get through very difficult times, although Mum would probably say that her strength also stemmed from her northern roots in Lancashire. Her self-discipline was second to none – except where cakes were involved, or throwing things away. She was a hoarder, especially where letters were concerned – a trait which I share. (Other traits include not folding things up properly in the airing cupboard, mismatching socks, and scrunching cereal packets together instead of using the flaps properly!)

They say that as one door closes another opens, and it did for Mum, because it wasn't long after I'd moved out of the flat that Mum met Ken and fell in love. We were all thrilled, especially when the news came that they were to marry in Barbados, where one of Mum's sisters 'Kath' lives. Mum and Ken went on to have a wonderful life together. They visited family and friends regularly, enjoyed many holidays abroad (Malta being one of Mum's favourite places), and worked tirelessly together in their involvement at

Thetford's Art Gallery – where Mum could indulge her love of art – before they moved on to the south coast.

Whatever Mum had going on in her life, she was never stroppy or haughty. It was important to her that people felt comfortable in her company, even strangers, and she was mindful of not causing offence. All she wanted was a good honest natter, but not to pry in any way. While out shopping, it was not unusual to find you were missing someone when leaving the shop, because Mum was still inside, chatting away with a sales assistant!

She always saw the funny side of things and wasn't afraid to laugh at herself – that was just one of her many virtues. Others included always taking the time to listen, offering encouragement, and being kind and thoughtful.

Mum loved socializing (all those people to chat with) – especially at barbecues with her friends, family, extended family, grandchildren, great-grandchildren, and pets, but thankfully never all at the same time – it could have been mayhem, but Mum wouldn't have minded, because she was a very tolerant and happy person.

Mum watched with great interest as her family grew and thrived. She kept in touch by phone or writing letters to everyone, which she so enjoyed, and would always make a point of saying how proud she was of us all. She knew that we were very proud of her, and now, sadly, she will be very sorely missed.

Tony's family have also had their share of grief in the last decade. First Tony's sister died, in her forties, from a brain tumour, then his father died soon after, and then later his dear mum, from a stroke, at the age of 83. It was a coincidence that Tony's mum died at the same age as mine from a stroke – two years and two months afterwards, to the day. Both our mums died the same week as our birthdays. We are both the youngest offspring. Our fathers had the same Christian name and both died at the age of 78. Tony has lost a sister and I have lost a brother. These coincidences are a comfort to us, because it makes us feel more accepting of these losses.

The only way I can understand life and death in a simple and light hearted way, is to think of us all on this conveyor belt which moves along through life. As newborns enter at one end, the elderly drop off the top at the other. This is the order of things, but there are those who fall off the side along life's journey, such as my dear friend Julie, Tony's sister, and my brother. There are different lengths of conveyor belt for different species of animal. The grief is still there when they go, regardless of time, but like the changing seasons, our perceptions die and then regrow into greater understanding and love – and, I like to think that we might meet up again in another place.

Just as with the two-legged family members, we started losing our four-legged ones, and what started out as headaches, when they became ill, ended up as heartbreak when we had to say goodbye. It was worse when the scenario was through old age rather than illness, because we had to decide when the time was right, and that's never easy or straightforward. Weirdly enough, most of my pets, including my cat Winston and my dog Gypsy, passed away at the end of October, which is a very spiritual time of year, and I took comfort from this, too.

Much happened in the first two years after Tony and I moved in, and mostly it involved works to the house – some exciting but most boring. We always tried to stick to our mid-week special meal to cheer us up. This was basically a special home-cooked meal and a bottle of wine to help us get through the week. Both our jobs were fine, and we really didn't get too much hassle from them, but I was aware that I had survived one round of redundancies and it was only a matter of time before the next round would come along. For the time being there was the endless list of tasks required on the house, and we seemed to be doing them at break-neck speed for fear of running out of money, a strange logic indeed – a bit like driving fast to the nearest petrol station because you're almost out of fuel! Anyway, we still managed to squeeze in a few holidays during this time. Our favourite place was Minorca, where we enjoyed all the things promised in the brochure – it was quiet, clean, safe, and an easy two-hour flight from Stansted.

Once we were looking at which side of the island we should stay at and found while looking at the brochure that we were saying, "Been there, been there, been there…" so we'd obviously gone there more than we realized! Although I had got over the many demons that had tormented me years before at the cottage, I still felt uneasy when I was sitting at the airport on my own for the minutes at a time that Tony would go off for the loo or whatever. I just hated the thought of getting lost and not knowing what to do, so there were definite insecurity issues still there.

Being married felt very natural and easy, so to be honest, the socializing side of life didn't appeal to me much. I considered all the things I brought to a friendship – which probably explained why they were few and far between. I didn't fancy going out in the evenings or doing excessive shopping; just the occasional outing or telephone, email, or text chat was enough. The one thing I did pride myself on was the keeping of confidences. I was always listening and offering advice where I could, and being positive with a genuine interest in the friend concerned.

Of course, I'd lost my beautiful, perfect friend Julie, who'd been my confidante and mentor. With someone else, I could enthuse about my latest stroke of luck or happy occurrence and have it met with a blank face or shrug of the shoulders, while when a story was told to me, I'd always show genuine interest at the good news. Often I'd come off the phone and think, "I'm not going to keep in touch any more", but I usually did – at arm's length now. Friendship is a funny thing – and so fragile it can sometimes break in a single action or conversation. This, I think, is why I enjoy the company of pets so much, as there's no hidden agenda, no misunderstandings, and no conditional affection. Their thoughts about you are simple, genuine, and constant.

There are so many other companions in our lives that we take for granted, and if you look around you'll see all the favourite things, old and new, which feed your soul and character. Whenever possible (not much time these days) I do try to indulge these or add to them. We seem to keep so much under wraps. Even if we can't incorporate everything into our lives, it's important to recognize what makes us tick– especially where work's concerned and all our focus seems to be on keeping our jobs and paying the bills.

By our third year at the house, Tony and I had decorated most rooms, and the external works were all finished. The garden had been blitzed from brambles and bushes, and new turf had been laid like an expanse of brand-new green carpet. It was all taking shape after a total of eight skips coming and going. (There would have been more, but we purchased a trailer in the end and had a tow bar put on the car – it did actually work out cheaper but meant more trips to the dump.) Inside the house there were still a few rooms to do, but we had definitely lost a lot of our initial gusto and were physically and mentally tired.

On top of our inertia there now came a request from my employers for volunteers for redundancy. I'd already survived one round of redundancies and now it seemed there were to be more, unless enough staff volunteered. At home, Tony and I went through all the pros and cons: obviously I'd have to get another job, preferably part time and local, because our dog and cat were reaching their twilight years and needing more care and attention (maybe a slightly convenient excuse on my part). This was an opportunity to rearrange our lifestyle, but we had to be mindful that the economic recession could make getting work very difficult. On the other hand, we would have the cushion of the redundancy pay to carry us along for a while, and I won't deny that, having been employed for the last thirty-three years, the thought of not going to work for a while was actually very appealing! So after discussing it with my boss and getting all the facts and figures, it became obvious that the pros outweighed the cons. After working my three months' notice, I left in spring 2010.

It's true that when you're out of a situation you can better see it for what it is, and I soon realized that this was the right decision. For a start, there wasn't the daily battle with traffic jams and delays, and the expense of paying to park the car was no longer an issue either. Even the social interaction within the office, which

I'd regarded as essential to my sanity, turned out to be nothing more than a sentimental whim compared to the company of my adorable pets and the birds, bees, and wildlife in the garden.

In the first week of being at home, I sat in the sunny conservatory with a coffee and heard the sound of nearby church bells. They were such a comfort, and I chose this as a sign that everything was going to be okay – even though it turned out that the church bells rang *every* Thursday morning (probably bell-ringing practice or something similar!).

Tony benefited as well from my constant presence in the home. The general rule before had been that the first one home would let the dog into the garden, feed the animals, and make our cups of tea. The second one home (normally me) would make the sandwiches for next day, cook the tea and do the dishwasher. Now I was happy to do everything, including decorating, gardening, and the pleasure of relaying to Tony all the things I'd done that day and who I'd spoken with or heard from. I occasionally had lunch with friends, but this became less frequent over time because I was mindful of not spending too much money at this stage. We had savings to fall back on, but only for so long and we still had so much to do on the house, including the kitchen. Ironically, if it had come to losing the house, we would have had trouble selling it because of its unfinished state.

The one thing I wanted to avoid was getting stressed and panicking about losing the house. However, my outlook on this seemed to change from week to week. Either I would take the pragmatic view: "What will be, will be" and "I/we will go with the flow", or I would be thinking: "I have to get a job this week! I'll do anything – as long as it's part time, local, not too low paid, free parking, nice environment", etc., etc., etc. The list seemed to grow all the time.

The weeks and months went by so quickly, and before I knew it, a year was looming since I had last worked. This was a really worrying wake-up call. I had applied for so many jobs online and in the newspaper; I had actually managed four interviews – even second interviews – but nothing of any significant promise. One friend suggested that I ask for feedback as to why I didn't get the jobs, but to be honest, I have no doubts that there are people much more qualified than me out there and having a wealth of experience doesn't really make a difference these days. Or maybe I'd put out the signals that this dreamy idealist would rather be at home writing a book!

Sometimes I'd wonder where this would all end. Much as I tried to be self-disciplined in searching for jobs, keeping house and home together, and keeping myself fit on the few bits of gym equipment we had, there were days when, I feel ashamed to admit, I could have stayed in bed and slept. Strangely enough, I never really watched daytime TV or went into the lounge at all other than to clean it, because by the time I'd got up, done various jobs, checked the email, searched for jobs, gone shopping and made a few phone calls, it was lunchtime. So after lunch I'd check the email again, type a few memoirs, feed the animals, make the sandwiches for the next day, prepare and cook dinner, and then Tony would be home again and we'd watch TV for the evening. Luckily we didn't have any yearnings to socialize in the evening unless we went out to eat; we were happy enough with our own company in our cosy home. Sometimes we wouldn't have the TV on and would sit and talk about things like the next stage of housey stuff and what my agenda was next (fair enough, as I was at home). One of the conversations which arose on a regular basis was about the furniture we had – there was too much for the house, and we needed to get rid of some of it.

When we had started life together we had enjoyed buying pine furniture, such as a dining set, bookcases and cabinets. Now it looked dated and bulky so we sold some of it on eBay. The pine dresser was to stay, though, because it was the first piece we had bought together and was very useful for storing and displaying so many things. So the dresser was staying, but the "rabbit hutch", as Tony called it, would have to go. It was a lovely old dark-oak washstand, but not especially refined, and I could understand that it didn't fit in anywhere – I used to use it for storing tinned food in my old kitchen, and I had good vibes from this little cabinet. Tony, unfortunately, didn't share my sentimentality, and I always tried to avoid this conversation, as he felt more than happy to throw it out. In my opinion, if there was one piece of furniture staying, it was this one – the jury was still out, as they say. Originally I had got it from a local auction room, as part of a lot with a standard lamp, for the bargain price of £22. The lamp had long since been thrown out, but the cabinet now housed all the photo albums.

Other conversations started with "When the pets die, we can…" (visit family more, stay out longer, have breaks away) – when I had a job! We agreed not to get any more animals once they were gone – not even a parrot, which Tony says he's always wanted. (I can't stand to see birds caged, anyway.) The pets were indeed in declining health, with dear little Mrs Wax, the cat, now using a dirt box indoors and sleeping most of the time. She had kidney disease and only months to live. The vet had been helpful in prescribing medication and special food, but there was only so much one could do.

Likewise, the dog, Rosie, was also on medication and special food to help with her inflamed joints. She managed to get around the house, but we had to help her get up and down the stairs each night and morning. Thankfully she slept throughout the night, but before the medication, we'd had to get up during the night to let her out into the garden whenever she needed to go, bless her.

To recap, here was I, 50 years of age, without a job, but with a 13-year old cat and a 15-year old dog (both of whom were on borrowed time), with limited finances (I know I was lucky to have any) and a house still needing much work to get it into a saleable state. It was fast approaching a year since I'd had last worked, and although I had strung out my redundancy money for as long as possible, there was no getting away from the fact that the situation would need to change very soon for the sake of our future stability.

To have come this far in the last thirty or so years and then see our hopes and dreams turn to dust as we paid our creditors didn't bear thinking about, and to be honest, I wasn't so sure I could cope with the frustration and panic of it all. Sorry to sound like a drama queen, but I was sold-out of *coping*. Clichés like "the darkest hour is just before dawn" and "trust fate" were creeping into my mind at night as I tried to calm myself to sleep; sometimes they worked, sometimes they didn't. At other times, to calm my nerves during sleepless nights, I would envisage all my emotions as wild horses running and rearing ahead of me. I'd grab their reins, hold on tight, and slowly draw them in towards me and so bringing the beasts under control. This seemed to work.

It's hard for me to comprehend that the 1980s were thirty years ago, because I still think of them as twenty years ago. Perhaps I'm reaching an age where I'm looking back at the past, thinking about the good old days when money was tight but never a massive issue, and employment was available in most quarters. Crime, drugs, and war didn't seem to appear so much in the news, and the weather wasn't so adverse – except for that hurricane in October 1987. I'd had more zest for life then and had tackled things head-on with all my heart and soul, but these days, by the time I've weighed up the pros and cons and considered just about every outcome, I can sometimes talk myself out of taking direct and immediate action. Plus I don't doubt that having a husband onside has allowed me to take a back seat on issues as and when it suited me. I also missed my mum terribly, particularly those cosy chats on the phone we used to enjoy, when I could air all my thoughts and she'd be completely understanding and say things to make me feel better. She seldom lectured me, except when she had a point to make – like my redundancy from working in London.

It's true that when you're out of work and trying to get a job, your self-confidence does take a knock from every unsuccessful application and interview. But even with these setbacks I still searched for jobs online, though this strategy appeared not to work. Then one day I saw a part-time vacancy advertised for an insurance administrator in a newly set-up office about eight miles away. The specification said that the hours could be negotiated, but the person was the most important aspect. I applied and sent my CV, then waited, ever hopeful, for a response. It came at last; I had an interview with a guy who had been a Lloyd's broker in the days when I used to work in London, so we had that in common. He now had his own business and was working from home, but he had decided to expand to this lovely office above a shop in a very old building. It would only be me and him initially, until he got more staff, but there was a space to park for free and the salary was good. Also, he was flexible on the hours, which equated to about twenty per week.

The interview lasted about thirty minutes, and I didn't know if that was a good thing or a bad thing, but it was on a Wednesday, and he said he would be making his decision on Friday. I was one of six interviewees from more than forty applicants – the recession was indeed biting hard. Anyway, I came home and kept high hopes that I'd get a phone call or email on Friday. But nothing happened.

It was difficult to put the job interview at the back of my mind, because I hadn't been told one way or the other, and I really had no idea what the outcome would be. We have a whiteboard in the kitchen for writing memos and reminders for food, etc., and daft as it sounds, I scrubbed out all the information and drew a horseshoe, four-leaf clover, shooting star, and rabbit's foot – and put a big V above them all! Well, it made me feel better.

I decided I'd have to make contact about the job on Monday at about 10.30 in the morning if I hadn't heard by then. I didn't, so I had to get in touch and leave a message asking for confirmation, if it was available, as I needed to know whether to continue my search for a job or not. After a few minutes, the phone rang, and it was the guy saying, "Sorry, Vanessa," (I waited for the inevitable, but he carried on) "but I've been so busy, and I'm glad you called because I'm writing to you today to offer you the position."

I couldn't believe my ears. I just kept thanking him and said that I'd be delighted to accept the job. We exchanged a few email messages to confirm prior to the letter. Then I spent the next half hour phoning everyone with the news. Of course, Tony was really pleased and relieved. Now I had just a week left at home before reclaiming my place back on that big wheel of industry again.

As you may have already gathered from the way I see things, there were coincidences involved here, and it wasn't only to do with all the lucky charms I'd plastered over the whiteboard. No, this office was actually a stone's throw from the picture shop where I used to work. Furthermore, my soon-to-be boss had mentioned in the interview that he intended to put his stamp on the place and maybe change his colour scheme, so as I like interior design, I could be useful. I didn't mention that I had worked close by and had painted the shop when I worked there. But the real coincidences came in the form of my new boss's name – it was exactly the same (bar one letter) as that of my late friend Julie's husband. Also, the boss had a dog he'd bring to work with him sometimes, named Max – the same name as Julie's family dog. The boss's dad had the same Christian name as Julie's dad, and the office was above a shop bearing the same name as Julie's mum. If ever I'd wondered if I was on the right path, this was surely a sign that I was. I was to start work on the last day of February 2011 – I had left my last job on the last day of March 2010.

Let this be hope and comfort to anyone who feels despondent about looking for work and not seeing anything suitable or not receiving a response to applications. Just hang on and keep the faith.

I still had much to prove, not least that I could cope after the amount of time that had passed since I'd last touched insurance work. But if it didn't work out, then it didn't work out – I could accept that.

On my first day, I felt completely out of my depth when I arrived at the office and found I had *three* telephones on my desk and a huge leather chair. I reckoned he must have had me down as some sort of executive, and I still had just enough humour in me to find this mildly amusing. By the time a few days had passed, I had found my way around the computer systems and procedures and had seen my boss for the man he was – a professional family man who ran his own business tirelessly. I admit I thought he should have employed someone a lot sooner, as there was so much work to do, but I could start to help now and draw on my many years of office experience – although, culturally, this was all very new to me working for one person. In any event, it was difficult to take it all too seriously when there was a seven-month-old cocker spaniel running around the place taking paper from the bins and ripping it to shreds!

The dog was not a permanent feature but an occasional perk, which was lovely. The boss, Philip, was in London at least once a week, so this allowed me the time alone to write notes and get to grips with the order of work. Having spent a year alone at home during the day and sorting out household finances, I found it helped me to now sit alone in the office and get on with business accounts.

After a few weeks, my confidence started to grow but there came a setback one morning when I arrived early for work on a day when Philip was to be in London. I was walking towards the office and saw a guy hanging around outside in the little courtyard. To my mind, he was loitering with intent of committing a crime, but of course this was just my interpretation. I didn't want to pass by him to get to the office, so I decided to walk around the block first in the hope that he would have gone by the time I returned. Not so lucky – he was still there. I started to realize that this might be a problem, as there was still no one around, so I walked around the block again, and this time I telephoned Tony, who promptly told me that I should "grow a pair" and walk past him, unlock the office, go in, and lock the door behind me. Well, excuse me for not growing a pair, but this advice was not helpful! Then while I was walking along, moaning back to Tony, the guy passed me going the other way. Great! I could now finish the phone call and get on with my life. As I approached the office for the third time, I realized the man was right behind me, so I swung around and said, "You're lost, aren't you?" (even though I actually meant "Why are you here?").

"I'm waiting for someone, and we're painting this property today," he said. Talk about conversation stopper. I wasn't sure how true this was, but suddenly a van stopped next to us, and a guy got out and opened the doors to reveal masses of painting paraphernalia – mystery solved and a massive sigh of relief from me! After that day, I discussed security measures with Philip, and we sorted out a proper alarm system and door security, which made me feel much safer.

The hours I worked proved to fit in well with home life, because I could be home around mid afternoon to feed our pets. Dear old Rosie was mostly asleep in her bed in the hall when I came home. I'd call her name, and as she woke I'd drop my bags and give her a big hug and kiss hello, secretly relieved that she was still with us. Then little Mrs Wax would appear, and I'd make a fuss of her, too, before letting Rosie into the garden and putting the kettle on for a cup of tea.

After feeding the animals and sorting our sandwiches for the next day, I'd start preparing dinner. I don't know how other people cope when children are involved – it must be a logistical nightmare. Nevertheless, I still used to feel a bit put out when people or Tony used to mention my part-time hours as if I put my feet up for the rest of the day, when in fact, when he got home from work Tony sat down long before I did!

Despite tiresome moments of trying to please people, I never felt my time spent on the animals was wasted. I knew Rosie wasn't long for this world, and I wanted to make her feel as comfortable and happy as possible. Her legs failed her sometimes, and she clearly suffered some days with aches and pains, but as long as her good days were more prevalent than her bad days, we did all we could to support her.

We knew the inevitable decision would have to be made at some point, and it was on my day off work that the realization hit home. Dear old Rosie. Her fifteen years showed as she lay in the garden that summer's day, occasionally sniffing the air, but otherwise motionless and weak. I spoke to Tony on the phone at lunchtime, and we agreed to make an appointment at the vet's for that evening. I once again marvelled at the many years I'd spent with Rosie and the comfort we'd brought each other. How fortunate that I'd spent the last year of her life with her virtually daily, just like Gypsy's final months – under different circumstances, with my illness, but precious time nonetheless. Now I faced the same inevitable loss and heartbreak, and I knew Tony would feel very much the same. We said our goodbyes to Rosie that evening.

The one thing grief teaches us is that it *really* hurts, but as daily life goes on regardless, a buffer seems to form, and the pain becomes less. I convinced myself that Rosie would be with Tony's parents and sister, and I would meet her again one day on the other side – along with Gypsy, Winston, Romie, Mr Pye, Violet the rabbit, and all the other pets that had gone before – and not forgetting all the people, of course, who I could hug again in the world beyond.

I find it strange that we can become softer and more loving every time grief strikes rather than harder and more bitter. I'd been in my job for four months, and

I felt adequately settled and knowledgeable about the work and my role. There was still much to learn, and I suppose I was a bit lazy about learning more, because I already had enough information to get me through the day. There was definitely a factor involved relating to keeping life on an even keel at all times, which could be tiresome. Anyway, when my boss said one day that he had booked a family holiday to America for two weeks, I woke up and smelt the coffee immediately!

Unfortunately, I'd already booked a week off work to complete the redecoration of our dining room – pale-pink painted walls and white wooden blinds at the windows to lighten the dark wood flooring and furniture. To soften the look, we had a light-coloured tapestry table runner and a long wicker fruit basket along the centre, and with a few vases of silk flowers in varying colours around the room and some specially selected pictures, the overall look was surprising charming. This was all very well, of course, but now it was tinged with the dread of knowing that I had just three days back at work before the changeover to Philip's holiday.

The time had come for me to knuckle down and get in the driving seat for once. So I did. I asked as many questions as possible, so that I fully understood the procedures. I then made notes about the notes, if necessary, and kept in mind the new office alarm system, which I'd need to get through and set every day – alone. It's true that the past insecurities I'd experienced and petty annoyances had not completely disappeared, and they still affected my self-confidence. I used to rely heavily upon my inner courage in order to accomplish anything required of me – and with good results. Now my courage was not as strong as it once had been, and I was more than aware of this.

So there I was, on the first day my boss was off on holiday, sitting at my desk, surrounded by printouts of my email messages, trying to understand what I was supposed to do next. I was not actually moving much but almost sitting in a state of shock. Yes, complete apathy had arrived, and it seemed it was here to stay! Then suddenly, without any prompting, I decided to give myself a mental talking to. "Are you just going to sit here all day panicking, or are you going to do some work?" I asked myself. "It's not as if Philip is completely out of reach – he did say to phone him if necessary, as it wouldn't be a problem." (Obviously I didn't want to contact the boss if I could help it.) So I got up from my desk, put the kettle on, put the radio on, opened the windows, scooped all the email papers up together, got a coffee, and then worked through, page by page, looking at my notes. I worked my butt off for the rest of the day – and it felt really good!

After that, I took each day as it came. I felt much more equipped to cope. Philip did call the office a few times to make sure everything was okay, so I could always run a few queries past him. I realized that my best was, in fact, good enough, and I did have what it took to succeed. This gave me a renewed sense of belief in myself. No, I wasn't ready to swan off to London on my own for a jolly day out yet – but the prospect wasn't as scary as before. This was a good gauge of my progress, as it was the last memory I'd had had before sanity had left me during that fateful journey home over a decade before.

But now Tony was very supportive of my new achievement, and he encouraged me by saying that he hadn't doubted my abilities for a second. By the end of the two weeks, which included working on my days off, the work was mostly up to date, with no howlers to report, and the office was polished and Hoovered, ready for Philip's return.

From then on, I seemed to put more and more effort into doing the work and less and less into the draining analysis of how I felt about it. We've all heard the cliché about giving ourselves a good talking to – and it really does work. I only wished I'd done it sooner. But now I was finding and trusting my own judgement (without the critical telling off), and it gave me great comfort.

Overall, life was good. The work–life balance was paying off, and we found time to go out on our bikes some evenings for a six-mile jolly and the feel-good factor that came with it. Sometimes Tony would cycle on ahead and I'd have trouble keeping up, but he always waited at some point. We'd go for meals at the pub or have a little barbecue on our own in the garden, which we enjoyed. Dear Mrs Wax was still going strong, though she would be prone to night-time sickness – and bless her, at least she managed to honk on the bathroom floor, so clearing it up wasn't too difficult. We got used to this occasional "blip", but the writing was on the wall – she wasn't getter any better but actually worse, and she would continue to do so. Inevitably we would have to decide when the time had come for yet another visit to the vet's – but not yet.

We took a chance and booked a house-sitter through a proper company to come and first meet Mrs Wax and then stay at the house and look after her for a week, so we could take a much-needed holiday abroad. It was October, and we knew it was unlikely that we would go somewhere really hot (long travel times, expense etc.), but we booked to stay at a hotel in Minorca and were surprised at how lovely the weather was. We spent almost every day on the beach, just soaking up the sun and having an occasional dip in the clear sea – it was absolute bliss and just what we needed.

Back home, everything was in order, and Mrs Wax was fine. We felt so relaxed; we really had benefitted from our break. Of course, our minds were still on our dear little friend, but she was doing well and had her bed (a fluffy cat igloo) firmly placed in front of the radiator, where it acted like a heat tent! When we went to bed, we wrapped her in her warm bedding and left her to sleep for the night. It may sound a bit drastic, but we simply wanted to spend every last second with her that we possibly could. Even when we were out of the house at work, we put the heating timer on, so that she didn't get cold during the day.

In March 2012 we had some amazing days of really warm sunshine, so Mrs Wax enjoyed a few hours in the garden on my lap, sunbathing with her front paws over one arm – she looked up at me adoringly with her expressive green eyes filled with bliss. There was no better way to spend time in the garden than like this, and I cherished every second.

There were a few more weekends like this to come, with unusually sunny weather and these special moments in the garden. But inevitably, everything changed, and within a few weeks, the day came when we knew we had to call the vet for an appointment the following day. The next morning, I noticed that several trinkets around the bedroom were sparkling in the morning sunlight. At that point, I decided that I would always be reminded of dear sweet little Mrs Wax every time I saw crystals of light, because that summed her up – a special ray of light. Even the sequins on my slippers sparkled, and this gave me comfort.

The afternoon was very sad and upsetting as we kissed our very special companion goodbye. She slipped away quickly and peacefully and suffered no more. We left the vet's with heavy hearts and hugged each other as we pulled ourselves together. As we got into the car, a woman walked past in front of the car. As she turned to face us, we saw that the top she was wearing had tiny gemstones, which caught the afternoon sun and sparkled brightly. I took this as a sign that Mrs Wax was with us again in spirit.

If ever there was justification to getting in through the front door and aimlessly mooching around the empty house, it was now, but it didn't happen that way – quite the opposite. Instead, Tony went straight to the airing cupboard and started changing the timer on the central heating, saying, "We won't be needing that on 'timed' anymore." I smiled. Normally I'd probably have laughed, but it was a true smile at the realization that there was always a silver lining to be had somewhere on these tragic occasions, and I was so glad he was mindful of our outgoing costs and global warming at this sad time!

My husband (as he's known at these times) also pointed out that we could now go and visit family – Trish and John in the Isle of Wight. Wonderful as the feeling of freedom might be, I did feel inclined to mooch for at least a week in due recognition and remembrance of our last remaining pet leaving the family fold. Tony obviously got over it a bit quicker than me and was definitely more pragmatic about things. Nevertheless, I was looking forward to our days of carefree folly and family visits, so we did book to go away for a few days. A visit was well overdue, as Trish and John had moved into their new home two years earlier and we hadn't seen it yet.

The April weather was completely different from March, and the wind and rain made for a hellish trip across the Solent. The ferry rocked from side to side, and the captain asked all passengers to remain seated in the interests of safety. (That was a laugh, because no one wanted to walk and be thrown around!) I was just glad we weren't sailing across the ocean, but I dare say there are plenty of adrenalin junkies who would have found it thrilling. Even Tony looked a bit green about the gills – and he doesn't worry about anything. Saying that, we are all works in progress, and our attitudes can and do change all the time – if we want them to.

Anyway, we arrived safely at Trish and John's, and after our hugs and kisses, we saw what a wonderful job they'd done to make their home so warm and welcoming on this wet and windy Sunday afternoon. The first things we noticed were the delicious smell of a roast dinner cooking and a log fire crackling in the lounge. Through the hallway, we spied a massive home-made chocolate cake sitting proudly on the kitchen table, and Trish was already making cups of tea, bless her. Tony and I looked at each other and winked in approval – it was obvious that our few days' visit was going to be a welcome change on every level and in every sense.

After the delicious roast beef dinner and sumptuous desserts (the cake was coming later) we relaxed with our wine and chatted in front of the fire. I marvelled at how similar we were as sisters, but of course we came from the same parents, who taught us the same values, so it wasn't really so surprising.

But we have two more sisters, and collectively there is not a constant or direct communication together but rather information passed on – it's just how it's worked out, because not everyone sees eye to eye, which is fair enough. Anyway, back to our Isle of Wight jolly. Just as we were getting settled for the evening, Trish and John mentioned that they usually went for a walk after dinner, and so there was no reason not to now – other than the atrocious weather outside! Luckily we all had good waterproofs with hoods, so we stepped out for our little jaunt. We seemed to march our way around the streets and parks – even negotiating a massive fallen tree en route. When Trish had said they sometimes walked for ten miles, I'd thought she had to be joking. Luckily we were only out for about an hour, which was long enough when you had to shout to be heard through the wind and rain. Maybe we're not as alike as I thought!

When we got back, we had a few cups of tea in front of the fire – and out came that fantastic, gooey chocolate cake, layered with fresh whipped cream and tasting every bit as good as it looked – bliss. Shortly afterwards we went to bed and slept like logs after our very long day.

The next morning, after tea, coffee, and a hearty cooked breakfast, we decided to go out in the car (yeah!) and do a few trips, which incorporated a craft centre and donkey sanctuary. The craft centre was a bit boring, and we just bought a few bits for home, but the donkey sanctuary was much more fun and brought a few laughs in itself: firstly, the weather – it was still grotty, and we were the only ones there. Secondly, the donkeys were completely disinterested! Despite our calling for their attention (there were about twenty to thirty of them in the field), three had their backsides against the fence and were not going to turn towards us, one was rolling on its back in the mud, another was following a rabbit around the top of the field (which was quite amusing), and two other donkeys were "at it"! So all in all, it was not like a previous visit years before. However, we did enjoy being there, and our time was spent together laughing. Food was a major part of our minibreak, so we went for a meal that evening at a nearby hotel restaurant. The food and wine were excellent (we took a cab so we could all drink). We discussed how friendly and helpful the doorman was – it turned out that he owned the hotel and simply enjoyed greeting and welcoming everyone to his hotel – which was a well-oiled machine and immaculately clean and efficient. He even took us and showed us where ducks nested on the grounds. Apparently they nested in the same place every year and had even brought their ducklings into the foyer in the past. We laughed, because duck had appeared on the menu!

The following day, we were heading for home. It was all too soon, but we had to leave because we had already arranged for an electrician to come in and start work on the kitchen. We vowed we'd be back to see them as soon as possible and would, of course, keep in touch in the meantime. The journey home gave Tony and I the opportunity to have a long chat about how and where *our* lives were going. Yes, we had workmen coming in again, as part of this quest to finish the house, but where were we going to move to, and would we want to move after spending so much money on the house?

Tony kept his pragmatic head on, as usual, and said, "Look, darling, nothing is set in stone – we could finish the house this year and move, or we could stay longer and enjoy it. We could move nearer your work, or we could move somewhere completely different and leave our jobs. Even the Isle of Wight is not out of the question, but I think it's more of a retirement option in our case, as there are so few jobs available."

Well, that summed it all up, actually, because nothing *is* set in stone, and while our jobs were massively important to us — I was especially enjoying mine — I was already thinking that if I had access to email, the files, and a telephone, I could do my job anywhere. But I *would* leave the company if it was absolutely necessary. Tony enjoyed his job too, but his constant travel made him so dependent on not getting caught up in traffic jams because this affected his task time for the day.

In any event, our house did not have to be pristine, just good enough to sell easily one day. Finding another home, preferably tucked away in an unspoilt stretch of the countryside somewhere, shouldn't be completely out of the question. Anything was possible, as I had come to learn, and what's more, magic and miracles *did* happen in real life. I had to trust in fate as well as my own instincts, because they appeared to be linked. There is no point in me trying to search for this peace of mind and wonderful life. No, this time it was a matter of waiting for utopia to find me.

I keep a little pocket diary next to my bed, in which I jot down the events of each day. I believe that each and every day is important, whether positive or negative, because it's a day to live and learn.

For the most part I feel blessed, and I know that — just as predicted once before by a clairvoyant — I do have a life to behold. I am also fortunate to have Tony in my life, because he is a special man, and I could probably write a book about him and all his many virtues – but not right now. Sometimes I fret that I may lose him one day, maybe to a better woman (believe me, there are plenty of better women), but as a soul-mate he has become a huge part of my world, and I couldn't love or appreciate anyone more – even though it's not always obvious!

A typical way we operate together would be easily demonstrated by this incident. One day there were a couple of coloured doves on our roof, cooing away down the chimney. We didn't mind, but we soon realized that they were trying to build a nest under the eaves of the roof – on the arm of the satellite dish. The TV reception was still okay, but there were a few twigs stuck in the dish mesh and even more twigs on the pathway next to the house. I felt a bit sorry for them, because there was no way a nest could be built on a narrow metal arm. I went to the shops, got a small rectangular basket, and asked Tony if he could fix it to the arm for the birds, to give them a head start on a safe and secure nest.

My request to Tony, however, was met by a very uncharacteristic response: "If you honestly think I am getting up a ★★!!?!!★★ ladder to fix a wicker basket for a bird's nest to our satellite dish, then you've got another think coming!" Well, I knew I didn't need "another think coming" because, by the end of the day, there he was, as I knew he would be, up the top of a ladder, fixing a basket to the satellite dish arm – and fixing it with plastic cable ties for extra strength!

The basket looked slightly strange, but it didn't show that much and didn't interfere with the TV reception, either.

The doves sat on the next rooftop, looking across at the instant nest. In time, they came back and added a few more twigs of their own. We could see the side of the basket if we looked out of a bedroom window, and it wasn't long before Mummy wasn't leaving the nest, so we checked out of the window regularly for any activity. One day there were two little beige, fluffy dove heads wobbling above the nest.

The chicks were very good and didn't try to leave the nest, which was a relief to us, as it was quite a long drop down. Eventually, of course, we looked out and saw two small doves perched on the sides of the nest, with their parents on the neighbour's roof calling to them to fly across. They didn't, but went back into the nest instead. The time wasn't right for them. The next day they tried again, and this time one managed to leave the nest and sit on our roof. Fortunately it was August, and the weather was fine. The following day, the other young dove flew onto the roof. They were now free, and the parents often joined them, which was nice to see. The youngsters still came back to the nest whenever they felt threatened by any rooks or other birds who took an interest.

It was a privilege to witness these marvels of nature, and I saw more at the same time, as we had a grey squirrel visit the garden for a few days running. It must have been a youngster, as it was quite small and slim; it looked healthy and had a magnificent fluffy tail. It was certainly active – apart from climbing up and down trees and arguing with a few young magpies within the foliage, it dug a few holes in our lawn to bury things! We don't have nuts, but there were obviously foodstuffs to be had. This little mite dug quite deeply, put something in the hole with its little paws, and then used the soil to pack back into place. It was fascinating to watch from the patio, and I sat as still as possible so as not to disturb it. I captured these special moments, because I'd taken a week off work to "chillax" after the three weeks in July I had covered the office and looked after Max while Philip went away on a family holiday to Costa Rica.

The dog-fostering situation came about when my work life was cruising along quite merrily – and by that I mean that work had become less of a constant worry in my mind and more of a relatively enjoyable way to spend the day as well as being something that paid. That's how it should be, I suppose. Anyway, I was probably in a very receptive frame of mind when the boss asked whether I'd look after Max while he was away. I could even bring him to the office each day. I said I'd ask Tony first before committing, which also gave me a bit of time to think seriously about the implications. I ran the idea past Tony that evening, and as usual, he was his easygoing self and said it was entirely up to me, as I'd be the one looking after him and taking him to work, though of course we could both walk him at weekends and play in the garden each evening. This was surely preferable to putting Max in kennels, as he knew me from his many visits to the office. So there was the answer, then.

Max was a lovely little dog – a two-year-old black-and-white cocker spaniel with gigantic paws, a black, curly mop of hair on his head, brown eyebrows, and brown muzzle and beard. He was full of fun and mischief in equal quantities, yet he also craved companionship, so he would certainly be getting that – 24/7! From our point of view, it would be good to have a pet about the place again. Looking after Max wasn't going to be a complete walk in the park, not least because, him being the boss's dog, we would have to look after him as if he were the crown jewels. This brought a lot of responsibility with it.

Tony and I got as prepared as possible. We fetched Rosie's old bean bag from the loft, dug out her old extendible lead, and found a few stainless-steel bowls in the shed – all in perfect order and impeccably clean, just as dear Rosie herself had been. The only thing we bought was a dog harness for the car, as I wasn't sure how he travelled and didn't fancy him jumping all over me while I was trying to drive. I needn't have worried, because Max turned out to be the most well-behaved dog ever in the car.

For the first week, we managed to structure a routine to accommodate walking, feeding, and taking Max to work, etc. For the most part it was working, but it was very tiresome for us. Max, on the other hand, seemed completely at ease about the whole set-up and quite enjoyed having a run around the garden and playing with toys each evening as we watched TV. By night he slept upstairs beside us, on the bean bag, and snored very loudly most nights! The biggest inconvenience I found was the amount of "number twos" he did, and I was constantly carrying black doggy bags in anticipation of the several I'd be using throughout the day. There was no making him wait, either – he would stop dead in the street and "go" – and the worst occasion was when we were right outside a hairdresser's window. There was no avoiding a spectacle as I cleared up in front of staff and customers within the salon. (I had had my hair cut there a few weeks before, but I decided not to go back due to the embarrassment.)

I had actually said to Tony after the first week that he should remind me to never get another dog, as they were too much like hard work! However, during the second week, as I had started to wise up to Max's wants and needs, I retracted my statement to Tony and decided that things weren't quite that bad. After all, it wasn't Max's fault that he had been lumbered with us to look after him for three weeks. There was no doubt that we were all starting to warm to each other. While Max hadn't been able to get on the bed when he first arrived, we didn't mind one morning on a weekend when we heard a scrabbling at the foot of the bed and then Max appeared right up at our faces, with his tail wagging and full of joy at his achievement. What could we do but give him a big cuddle while he laid on his back between us, just as Rosie used to do? He was such fun, and during the third week we were actually feeling a bit sad that he would be going home.

On the day Max went home – a little heavier than when he arrived, it must be said – we knew we would definitely be getting another dog, as well as two cats, though we were not sure exactly when. It would not be immediately, as we still had the house to finish and holidays to take. For now, though, we'd made a little difference in a dog's life, and his owners and family were relieved that he was okay. The office had operated just as well too, with no howlers to report. Max would, of course, be making an appearance at the office occasionally, so that was something to look forward to. I still had a pocket stuffed with mini black bags for those just-in-case moments!

It was getting towards Christmas 2012, when the boss suggested we go for a special Christmas lunch aboard the Orient Express train for the 3 of us and our partners. Initially I was so surprised by both his generosity and the prospect of the trip. We would travel to London on one train, spend four and a half hours on another – albeit luxurious and almost 100 years old – and then come home on another train. It had been a long time since I'd travelled this way, and now I was to spend most of the day on trains. As always, there was a plus point, and this was that the invitation extended to Tony so this was a great comfort to me. No amount of visualizing about how the day would go could reflect the actual reality, so I accepted gracefully, went and brought a new frock, and set about looking forward to the occasion – just as any normal, appreciative person would do.

The day came, and the weather was absolutely perfect – cold but sunny and bright. We left from London Victoria station, and I felt quite relaxed about the whole thing. The journey was to take us down to the Kent coast passing through Maidstone and Ashford before heading back on a sort of loop through Broadstairs, Faversham and Chatham. The dramatic scenery was absolutely beautiful, with fields and hills of green and frosty landscapes – we could have been anywhere. The carriage we travelled in was named Zena, and a bit of blurb on the leaflets informed us that "she" had been rescued in the 1960s and restored. There were highly polished wooden panelled walls and giant springy wing chairs which were wonderfully comfortable. We each had a window seat on either side of a table with an ornate lamp and curtains either side of the window. The five-course meal was served by finely dressed waiters and included smoked salmon, pumpkin soup, stuffed guinea fowl, chocolate roulade, and various cheeses, topped off with coffee and mince pies. We were *very* full!

Most importantly, the company was excellent and our conversations were as fast flowing as the train itself. This experience was new to all 6 of us so we could enthuse together about how amazing this trip was. We had mutual respect for one another and shared a sense of humour so laughed quite easily too. I had anticipated that there might be triggers to activate panic within me but actually as I felt so relaxed and happy, the triggers were not activated. This was a truly memorable day for all of us so three cheers for a very generous and thoughtful boss.

In some respects, this closed the chapter on my life that revolved around the commute to London by train each day. Yes, I will go to London again, maybe on my own, but I know it's not the problem it used to be – and furthermore, it's not necessary. Do I really want to squeeze amongst hundreds of other people, spending a fortune on the fare and experiencing delays and cancellations, when I don't have to? Of course not.

Shortly after this amazing experience, Tony and I came down with a really bad bout of influenza, along with most of the population. This flu was particularly horrible, and the night sweats and constant coughing meant we had little sleep and felt wretched with exhaustion. We were both on sick leave from work, and coupled with the cold, ice, and snow outside, it made for a very sorry state of affairs. Even with each other's company, daytime TV, and regular phone calls from well-wishers, I started to feel very depressed, alone, and isolated. Even more worrying, I was feeling detached in thought and action, just as I had fifteen years earlier. Such was the similarity – the feelings of panic were becoming stronger and stronger – that I started to dread the outcome, over which I seemed to have no control. However, by a sheer miracle, I had one really good night's sleep of ten hours – we both did – and the next day I was able to rationalize the situation, which went something like this. "Note to self: you've been very ill with flu for weeks; you're tired, fed up, unfocused, missing the pets you grieved for in the last year; you have no incentives, and now your spirits are as low as they can get – *but it will pass!* You know this, because it passed before, and so it will pass again – and this time will be much easier because you have the past experience to draw on." The mental note made perfect sense, and I took great comfort from it and felt so much better. I knew the situation wasn't entirely down to a mere physical illness and a few hard times thrown in. No, this was a wake-up call for change and ensuring my emotional needs were met – just like before. But this time I understood the remedy required, and I felt more in control already.

Maybe it wasn't a life-changer, but the first decision I made involved getting a pet back in my life, a creature I could care for and give a loving home to. I searched online and ended up at the cat rescue centre website, where I'd gotten Mr Pye and Mrs Wax all those years ago. I looked at all the cat photos and blurbs about their individual personalities and likes/dislikes. It was sad that there were so many but uplifting to think that maybe they would all eventually be happily placed with good families.

I was just about to leave the site when I clicked on the last name, which was Foster, and saw a close-up of a cat's face. He looked like a tabby, and the blurb beneath read:

> Foster is a tabby/white chap around
> 18 months old. Foster couldn't cope in his
> previous home, as it was too lively and busy

for him. He finds the world a bit daunting so needs someone who is happy to take life at Foster's pace! Once Foster knows you, he starts to show his chin-rub-loving side; he does love his fusses. We feel Foster needs to settle into a new home before he will show himself off, as a busy cattery environment isn't allowing him to really show his character. Foster needs a quiet and calm home with someone who won't pressurize him or have too-high expectations of him in the first few weeks/month(s).

Well, I could certainly relate to his plight and felt a definite buzz in my stomach at the prospect of Foster in our lives – though I'd have to clear it with Tony before making a decision. So a few days later, I broached the subject to him. I needn't have worried – Tony just said, "Darling, if you want a cat, we'll get a cat; you don't have to explain. I know how much you miss the animals, so it's no problem." What a top man!

Without further ado, I emailed the rescue centre and we arranged a meeting with Foster the following weekend. Tony and I were, thankfully, over the worst of being ill and were back at work.

Within a week of meeting Fozzie, as we call him, we arranged to bring him home. He was a little nervous at the cat rescue centre, and now at home he was absolutely petrified, poor thing, and just stayed under the hallway cabinet for the first half hour. We decided to lift the cabinet up and take poor Fozzie upstairs to the front bedroom, where we had all his food, bed, dirt box, and a few toys. We didn't close the door completely but left it ajar so he could come out when he chose.

I wondered whether I'd done the right thing, but time would tell. That night I heard a little cry from the landing, and so I called to Foster, and he came into our room and up to my hand and let me stroke him. I knew we'd be all right at that point. I lifted him onto the bed, and he settled straight away. It was quite uncanny how much he looked like Winston. He had a tabby coat, white socks, white bib, and snip of white on his nose, but there the similarity ended, because Winston had been a bruiser, and Fozzie was a big, loving softie who did, indeed, love his cuddles.

Over the next few weeks he made his way around the house and conservatory. (We locked the outer cat flap, as it was too soon to let him out yet.) He played around the house, slept on our laps, and adopted a chair in the lounge nearest the fire, where he'd sprawl out on his back with his feet overhanging the arm – so no sign of nervous tension there, then!

Another impulsive idea occurred to me. This time it involved Tony, who had shown a deep tolerance of my whims of late. Tony had been wanting a motorbike for years, and I had always put him off because I was fearful of losing him in an accident one day. But now, as it seemed to be time for change, I said, "Darling, if you want to get a motorbike, we'll get one – because I know how much you miss having one." To see the sparkle in his soft brown eyes made the decision so much easier and natural. I might have used his very same words, but I offered them with sincerity, and he knew this. So, like me, without further ado, he went online, looking at which motorbike to buy. Even though the prospect was scary, it felt like the right thing to do, so there were no feelings of panic or wretchedness.

It occurred to me that we had the cat that looked like Winston and a motorbike, just as in times past – all we needed now was a smaller old-fashioned house in a semi-country setting, and we'd be living the dream. It was early March, and life had the echoes of those early years in Essex.

The good things in life were once again returning, like old and trusted friends from the past. These favourite things and simple pleasures included time out from work at lunchtimes, when I'd enjoy a browse around local shops looking at antiques, pictures, works of art, books, etc. Occasionally I'd meet friends for a chat over lunch, but whether alone or accompanied, my spirits were lifted.

While I didn't have a burning desire to get a motorbike again myself, I was happy to ride pillion – in fact, I felt so happy I wanted to wave at everyone! (I didn't.) Our first trip out was to Finchingfield, where we stopped for a pub lunch and sat for a while on the bench outside the church. It was a lovely, sunny March day, heaven sent, and I said "thank you" in my mind to life on this fortunate occasion. I was now accepting of my destiny, and I understood my own vulnerabilities. By a strange contradiction, this awareness of right thought made me feel much more in control.

Someone once said to me, "We all get wobbly moments in life." Well, this is probably true, but up until fifteen years ago, I didn't get wobbly moments, ever. In fact, I used to go through life happy and carefree, until I discovered something about myself which had really shocked and saddened me. There seemed to be layer upon layer of different emotions which I hadn't been aware of and so hadn't considered.

From this discovery, I then found it difficult to forgive myself for my ignorance and self-neglect, which had created the situation leading to my illness. As a result, I felt on trial in front of my master (or spiritual) self.

It seemed as if the huge emotions had taken over the controls whilst my mind had to take a back seat, until it was found to be wise enough to lead once more.

If I could have read a book by someone who had gone through a similar experience, I might have found comfort and further support to help me through my darkest days. This is why I have written *this* book, and if it comforts one person, in the absence of my being there to hold his/her hand and reassure him/her that the confusion *will pass*, then so much the better.

I have no regrets, and I have asked myself the ultimate question: "If I could backtrack and stay on the road I was on, without the long and painful experience I went through, would I swap back?" My honest answer is a definite *no*.

From the darkness came the realization that I had found a "reality" in existence, in the form of an internal *Forever Home*, where living within it and caring for it were all that mattered. From this place came genuine beauty, strength, power, peace, and love.

Now I have become the person I deserve to be, and everything has fallen into place – despite the all-terrain detour!

Quite simply, relationships are going well with Tony, family, friends, and colleagues. My job is as good as any career prospects I could ever have dreamed of, and I enjoy life's simple pleasures such as having cheese on toast and a piping hot mug of tea on a rainy afternoon whilst reading a magazine, baking a Victoria sponge cake, listening to music (and dancing all the cake calories off), pottering around the home, sunbathing in the garden, cuddling the cat, writing letters to distant friends, mooching around shops for housey stuff, and generally feeding my soul.

I did all these things before, but now I make time for them because I understand how important they are if my life is to feel balanced. I appreciate the here and now, the events, the places, the people, and the animals who enhance my life, whilst I remember the events, the places, the people, and the animals who have gone before.

For me it took a long time, but once I had trust in both my mind and intuition, new insights emerged, and life began to make more sense.

A testing situation occurred recently when Tony and I had found a small cottage for sale in a beautiful location, with views of fields from three sides, and from the fourth, the sight of a tiny medieval church. Yes, it was absolutely idyllic, but after many hours of talking and three sleepless nights, we concluded that the cottage wasn't for us – we couldn't say exactly why not, it just didn't feel right. I slept soundly that night.

It really doesn't matter where we end up living or what the place looks like. What matters is that we pay attention to our intuition and trust that fate will take us to wherever we need to go. There will most likely be scary events along the way as we take many leaps of faith into the unknown but these will keep the fires burning brightly in a *forever home within* that's filled with peace and satisfaction.

About the Author

Vanessa Bunting has a professional career background which spans more than three decades.

She has written various articles for many magazines and newsletters.

This is her first book.

Vanessa lives with her husband and cat in Essex, England.